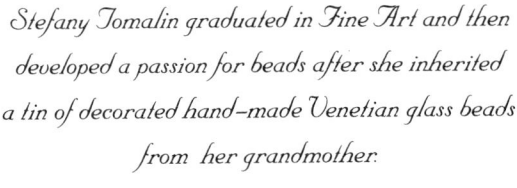

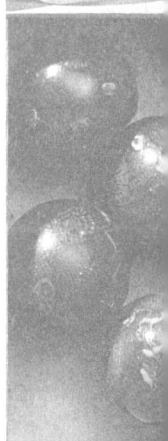

Stefany Tomalin graduated in Fine Art and then developed a passion for beads after she inherited a tin of decorated hand-made Venetian glass beads from her grandmother.

Unable to find any information on the subject, Stefany taught herself the skills as a designer, jeweller and collector. While bringing up a young family, she joined the craft fair circuit until the opportunity came to open her own shop in Portobello Road, London, in 1982.

She writes and lectures on all aspects of the subject and is one of the founder members of the Bead Society of Great Britain. Her first book, 'Beads!' has been consistently reprinted since its publication in 1988.

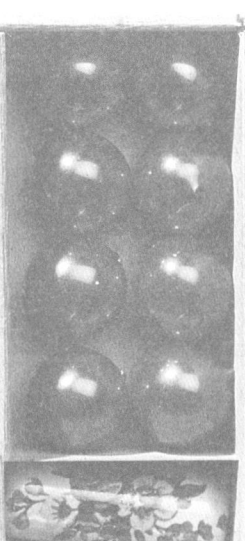

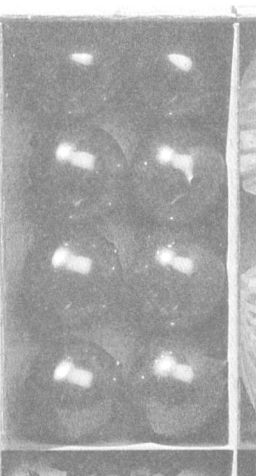

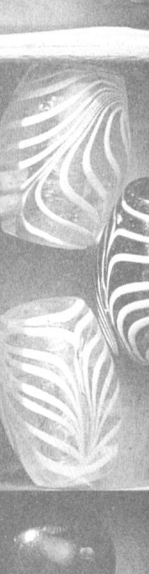

Bead Jewellery
WORKSTATION

STEFANY TOMALIN

WORKSTATION *is a new concept comprising
all the elements you will need to commence
the craft of Bead Jewellery.*

*The first 48 pages of this book offer a full-colour
introduction to Bead Jewellery, including
a selection of projects that will guide the user
through basic skills to more advanced techniques.*

*The remaining 16 pages at the back of the book
are printed with grids and templates and can be
used to create your own designs.*

DOLPHIN PUBLICATIONS

A DESIGN EYE BOOK

This edition specially produced in 1993 for Dolphin Publications,
Bridge Mills Business Park, Langley Road South, Pendleton, Salford M6 6EL,
by Design Eye Publishing Limited, 8 Fouberts Place, London W1V 1HH.

© Design Eye Holdings Ltd.

All rights reserved. No part of this publication may be reproduced,
stored in a retrieval system or transmitted by any means, electronic,
mechanical, photocopying or otherwise, without the prior written
permission of the copyright holder.

ISBN 1 872700 13 6

Manufactured in China by Giftech Ltd.

Illustrations by Harry Harrison
Photography by Paul Forrester
Chas Wilder
Cover photograph by Michele Rogers

Contents

INTRODUCTION *4*

COLLECTING BEADS *6*

TOOLS & BASIC TECHNIQUES *8*

IDEAS FOR BEGINNERS *14*

BEADWORK *22*

MAKING BEADS *32*

PROFESSIONAL THREADING *36*

FURTHER IDEAS *42*

ACKNOWLEDGEMENTS & SUPPLIERS *48*

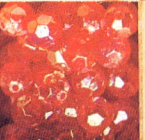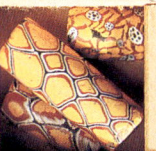

INTRODUCTION

Why do we wear beads? Not only because they add to the beauty of the wearer but also because they give enormous delight as a collection of small personal treasures in their own right! The technology is simple and the range of beautiful materials wide enough to include the commonplace and the most precious. Whether it's made of shell, wood, metal, plastic, ceramic or glass, coral, jet amber, pearls or gemstones, it is the size, colour, detail, significance and rarity of each individual bead, as well as the complete strung piece of jewellery, that provide so much scope. You can be sure there will always be some variety of beads in style, whichever way fashion may lean.

While taste and styles of adornment may change, there is no doubt that it is a fundamental human need – as strong as that for survival – to embellish, order and beautify both our surroundings and ourselves. Archaeologists show us that small items hung around the necks of even our most remote ancestors. Anything from animal claws, teeth, small fossils and shells to pebbles with natural holes, and, later, carvings in the softer durable materials such as wood, bone, amber or jet, have all been found in burials dating from around 30,000 BC!

Through the ages, beads have been endlessly adapted to suit different requirements – for counting, as dowry, to aid in prayer, to celebrate a land deal, even to protect babies from a sore throat or the evil eye!

Some of the most exquisite antique and modern beads are made by hand from glass that used to be dismissed as a substitute for more precious materials. This has all changed since the liberation of costume jewellery this century. Beads are no longer merely ephemeral or second best, for while ingredients may not be rare, they offer scope for individuality without limits of class or price.

· INTRODUCTION ·

Beads are also light in weight, virtually indestructible, colourful, replaceable and re-usable in new designs over and over again. They can easily be threaded and rethreaded, or they can be a permanent expression of highly developed and imaginative artistry. Some single beads are priceless miniature masterpieces.

In the pages that follow, you can learn the techniques of straight threading, earring, bracelet, and multistrand necklace construction, traditional knotting between beads, and take your first steps into the world of beadwork in lacy patterns and beadweaving.

The kit provided with this book has the ingredients you need to get you started on several of the projects, and these are the sorts of beads that are not difficult to replenish.

The first three projects are a useful introduction to the range of possibilities with beads. The projects that follow are developments and variations. All are intended as guidelines and inspiration for you to adapt your own individual designs.

This book shows you simple techniques for beautiful threading and beadwork, and you can also enjoy creating your own beads. The necklace and choker shown here are entirely composed of elaborate 'Fimo' beads, handmade and threaded by Akiko Kase.

Collecting Beads

As you start threading, you will probably find yourself hoarding old broken jewellery, obtaining bits and pieces from family and friends, peering in as you pass charity shops, and taking a serious interest in jumble and car boot sales. Before you know it, you'll be hooked!

Collecting individual beads is an exciting hobby in its own right. There are many advantages. You will be able to create a significant collection even if you are only spending pennies at a time. The variety of beads in circulation is enormous. Beads almost never deteriorate and, as the materials from which they are made have little intrinsic worth, they are unlikely to attract theft. The collector can enter the worlds of remote antiquity, of minerals and stones, of theatre costume, of collectable early and recent plastics. He or she can learn about glass techniques, country crafts, join the nostalgia craze for Victoriana or Art Deco, find out about the wonderful ethnic crafts of many peoples across the continents, or even concentrate on the beads used for trading, counting or praying.

Almost every local museum all over the world will display some beads of historic or local interest, and antique markets provide an opportunity for enquiry and hands-on observation.

And, of course, the extra bonus of a bead collection is that you can wear it!

• COLLECTING BEADS •

STORING YOUR COLLECTION

If you intend to be a serious collector, all specimens should be labelled as soon as they are acquired, with details of anything you know about them. The most important information will be:

- *Material.*
- *Visual description, including dimensions and condition.*
- *Date of manufacture, if known.*
- *Place of manufacture, if known.*
- *Where purchased and when.*
- *How much you paid.*
- *Any references in books. Experts will tell you that a good look at the inside of the hole can give vital clues to origins.*

If you buy a string to take apart and keep some for your own collection, it may be useful to describe the string it came from. If loose among items in, say, a sewing box, then make a note of what it was with. This will help establish a date.

Bead collections happily fit into shallow boxes with compartments, small old-fashioned stationery drawers, dentist's cabinets, old-fashioned card index drawers, old print trays, or even boxes for chocolate assortments which have ready-made little hollows in the trays to protect your pieces.

A collection of beads can be kept and attractively displayed in an old print tray.

CHAPTER
• ONE •

Tools & Basic Techniques

Unlike other jewellery techniques, working with beads requires only a minimum of preparation. You probably already have most of the equipment at home, and there are only a few essential skills to master such as the knots shown in this chapter.

Preparation & Equipment

Most of the indispensible tools you need will be found in your sewing box, manicure set or household toolbox, as listed below. If you want to do beadweaving seriously, it is well worthwhile to purchase a good beadloom with rollers at each end to accomodate extra warp length, as fully described in Chapter 3. Likewise, if you wish to concentrate on making beads yourself, there will be some additional equipment which is listed in Chapter 4, but the most important ingredients are good eyesight, clean hands, and plenty of enthusiasm. The kit provided with this workstation gives enough materials to get started on the techniques, and make several projects. However I am sure you will begin to accumulate your own stock of favourite beads to choose from – not only newly bought ones but also beads from old and broken necklaces.

WORKING AREA The ideal place to work is on a tray, as work may have to be moved while in progress. Many professional designers use a grooved

An assortment of useful and familiar tools ready for working.

tray or "bead board", as it makes it simpler to lay out your beads in a symmetrical sequence and see what the necklace will look like before it is threaded up. Pearl knotting is often done on a piece of velvet to prevent the beads from rolling about before they are threaded.

While working, pour small quantities of beads into shallow china or glass dishes such as saucers or ashtrays. These are better than yoghurt pots, which tip over too easily. When doing any work with the tiny *rocailles,* you will be able to plunge your needle in at an angle and scoop up several on it at a time.

BEAD STORAGE You will find that the best containers for storing your beads for use will be clear jars with screw lids such as jampots and babyfood jars, keeping the colours sorted, dust free and visible.

Beads on strings can be hung as room decoration until you are ready to use them. Rows of hooks, or an individual hook over a window are ideal for displaying a splendid set of beads to advantage.

As with beads, reels of thread also need to be protected from dust. If you wrap them in cling film or clear freezer bags, you will still be able to see all the colours.

BASIC TOOLS The advantage of this craft is that most of the equipment is neither unusual nor expensive and you may already have several of the most useful tools at home. All you need is some fine sewing or manicure scissors; a pair of small "round nosed" jeweller's pliers; at least one darning or knitting needle; a tape measure; wire cutters; and some matches. If you do any work with wire, you will also need a second pair of jeweller's pliers. While the round-nosed type are best for making the loops at the ends of the wires for earrings, snipe-nosed pliers are the best shape for gripping and bending angles. Additional tools such as tweezers and a scalpel will always be useful, while the more specialised equipment for drilling and modelling your own beads is described in the chapter on making beads.

Tools & Basic Techniques

BEADING NEEDLES Fine beading needles are essential for many of the projects in this book that involve *rocaille* beads and beadwork. The needles generally come in packs of assorted sizes 10-14, the higher numbers being the finer ones. They don't last very long so you will need a good supply.

Some of the necklace techniques in the projects do not need regular beading needles because they are worked with thicker thread, and by using a needle made of a folded over length of fuse wire as shown, a neater method of finishing off is possible, as the needle can be removed without cutting the thread.

Beading needles   *Home-made fuse wire needle*

Safety note – beading needles are dangerously sharp, so any broken ones must be gathered and taped or wrapped before disposal.

THREADS Several projects in this book require the best and strongest proper flexible thread. **Bonded nylon thread,** which comes in several thicknesses and colours, is available only from specialist suppliers. '40' thickness is the most versatile, '60' and '80' for work with tiny beads in beadwork or on the beadloom, and for items like threaded earrings which won't have to carry too much weight. A fairly good substitute is strong **polyester sewing thread.**

Traditionally, **silk thread** was always used for pearls but, like other organic fibres, it perishes with time. Delicate beadwork used to be done with a very fine **linen thread**. **Round hat elastic** is used for the bracelet project. **Leather thonging** is popular for large holed beads, or **braided or twisted cord.**

Avoid nylon fishing line (also known as monofilament, gut, or

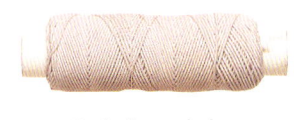

Reel of round elastic

Spools of nylon thread

Thick waxed braid

Leather thongs

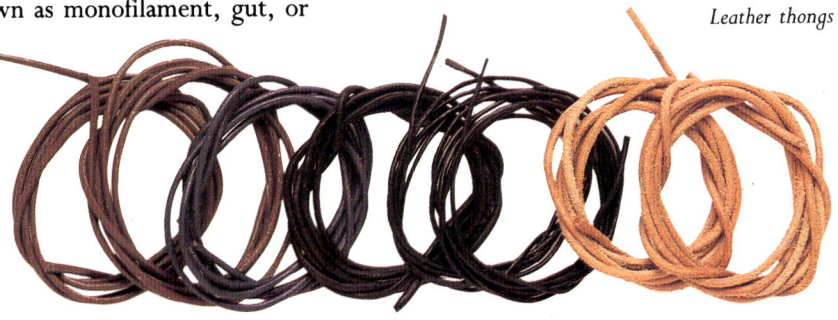

transparent thread). Although you can easily push it through the beads without a needle, it never hangs well, knotting is unsatisfactory and it can snap without warning. It is easier to push real thread through without a needle if the end is stiffened with nail varnish and trimmed to a point.

Beeswax will strengthen any thread that is rubbed along it. This minimises fraying and tangling and is recommended for all the techniques of beadwork.

Jewellery Wire – Sterling silver or silver plated copper, in 22 SWG (.7mm) or 24 SWG (.56mm) is needed for freedom with earring making, as in the project on page 16. Otherwise you can use the ready-made lengths called **'headpins'** (wire lengths with a knob resembling a pin head) or **'eyepins'** (with a small ring bent at one end). Most suppliers stock these along with the other small ready-made jewellery attachments known in the trade as 'Findings'.

FINDINGS Every bead shop, hobby or craft supplier has a range of inexpensive metal components finished in silver plate or gilt, and they may be bought singly or in small packs. They include clasps of various types, such as barrel screw fasteners, push snaps and bolt rings, brooch backs, spacer bars, jump rings (these form links for assembling wired units but are not suitable for thread because the ring is not closed and thread can pull out), split rings to partner the bolt rings, and earring hooks and clips in a variety of designs, known as shepherd's crook, kidney wires, posts and butterflies, and so on.

If you have a problem with allergic reactions to the metal hooks, choose surgical steel, sterling silver or gold.

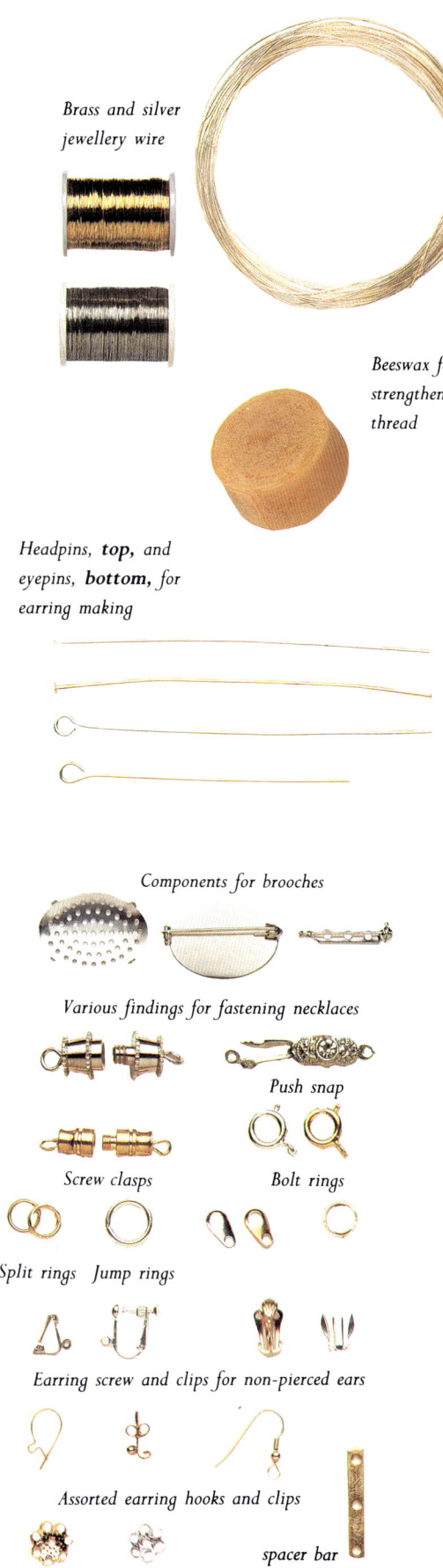

Brass and silver jewellery wire

Beeswax for strengthening thread

*Headpins, **top**, and eyepins, **bottom**, for earring making*

Components for brooches

Various findings for fastening necklaces

Push snap

Screw clasps   *Bolt rings*

Split rings   *Jump rings*

Earring screw and clips for non-pierced ears

Assorted earring hooks and clips

spacer bar

Filigree bead cups

GLUE Good threading and knotting should make the use of glue quite unnecessary, but with some awkward jobs the only way to secure the final knot may be with the tiniest touch of glue. Use an ordinary quick-drying transparent glue and keep it away from the beads.
(Superglue is a menace. It will run into the bead holes, immobilise the thread and block up the beads, which will then need drilling to be usable again.)

GIMP 'Gimp', 'bullion' or 'purl' are names for the special tiny coils of wire that protect the thread where it goes through the fastener loop. It may be available in silver, or silver gilt, in more than one thickness from specialist professional suppliers of pearl-threading requisites. The medium size is thin enough for your doubled thread. It can be cut to the necessary lengths with small scissors. Take care not to pull it, because although it resembles a coiled spring, if stretched, it will not resume its original shape.

Gimp is sometimes hard to obtain. It may be possible to salvage the pieces from an old necklace. You'll need to remove it carefully without stretching.

Small lengths of gimp

Basic Techniques

Making bead jewellery involves very few skills or tricks. Special methods for some of the jewellery are shown with the projects, but for all techniques using thread, there are a few reliable knots that are used in almost all the projects and are worth making sure that you know, because with the wrong knot your work will quickly collapse. Many people assume that knots will be stronger if you tie another one on top. This does not help, and in bead threading, any knots form part of the appearance of the finished necklace and should be discreet.

SLIP KNOT This is a temporary knot tied at the ends to prevent beads sliding off while you work, but can easily be untied when you are ready to finish off. It looks rather like half a shoelace bow.

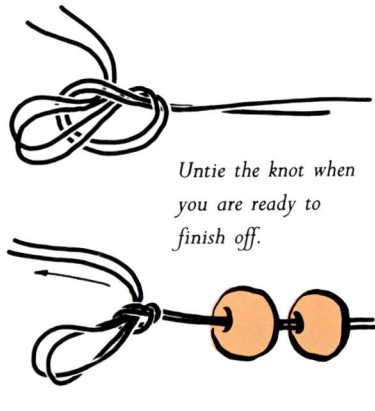

Untie the knot when you are ready to finish off.

LARK'S HEAD Tied with the loop at the end of a doubled thread or cord on to the ring of a pendant or any other attachment if appropriate, it has many uses in bead threading and jewellery and looks both simple and elegant.

WEAVER'S KNOT In beadwork and beadweaving, a knot is required for joining threads in the middle of the work that will be inconspicuous and slim enough to slide inside a bead if possible.

OVERHAND KNOT Using two strands, four strands or more tied in the way shown, with any number of strands, this knot is much less likely to let you down than the usual reef knot. It is tightened by separating the strands into two bunches and pulling them away from each other quite hard.

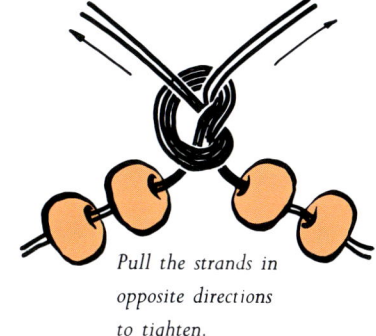

Pull the strands in opposite directions to tighten.

SEALING A FINISHED KNOT made with the nylon thread. This prevents a knot at the end of a necklace from unravelling or working loose. Once you have made it as tight as you can with absolutely no slack at all, cut the ends close to the knot, with the shortest amount of 'whiskers' protruding. Hold the work up so that the whiskers point upwards. With your other hand, hold a lighted match just above and watch the fibres of thread melt gently into a small blob. The exact amount of singeing can be controlled by removing the match as soon as you have melted enough, and you can dab it out with a moistened fingertip or wet cotton swab. This works like sealing wax on a parcel. With other threads, you may have to use a tiny dot of light glue.

Using a match to melt the whiskers and seal the knot.

Safety note — *supervise children while matches are being used, and always make sure the match is extinguished before dropping it in the bin with all the thread offcuts!*

CHAPTER TWO

Ideas For Beginners

These initial projects are not very difficult to do and show more than one interesting technique. They require the kinds of beads that are usually easiest to obtain: small glass beads in many colours as supplied in the kit, or beads with larger holes of glass, wood, metal or plastic.

Rocailles

Round embroidery beads, also known as ***rocailles*** or seed beads, are the smallest glass beads, made traditionally since at least the 15th century, by blowing a molten glass bubble and pulling it out to form a very long narrow tube of coloured opaque or transparent glass, which is then cut into a great number of sections and rounded off by a heat-polishing process.

Today, ***rocailles*** are made in Italy, Japan, the Czech Republic, France and India. The standard sizes range from 5mm diameter (about 1/4in) down to less than 1mm, but the tiniest are no longer produced. For your Love Beads, below, a variety of sizes together may be more attractive.

Tubular embroidery beads are made in the same way but cut into longer lengths. They are usually called 'bugles'.

Embroidery beads available today have a variety of finishes: they may have a pearly, metallic or iridescent coating over the glass colour, or be clear with colour or silvering inside, and bugles especially are often finished with surfaces faceted longways to increase the sparkly effect for evening gowns and trimmings encrusted with bead embroidery and sequins.

Because some colours are hard to find or expensive, such as the best reds, pinks and purples, techniques have been developed for dying beads, which involve dipping them in a coloured varnish. The drawback is that the colour is not permanent and may come off with any washing or dry cleaning, or may even dissolve with the application of perfume! Many of the old 'twenties dresses that were heavily beaded now have a faded appearance because they have been washed.

Hippy Love Beads

In the 'sixties, the Flower Children discovered peace and love, and bedecked themselves with accumulated strands of tiny, multi-coloured beads which were so pretty and inexpensive that they could be freely given and exchanged with anyone you fancied. Once again, they fit perfectly with the eclectic fashions of today.

The loop should be long enough to put round your neck more than once. The weight is very light and many strands can be worn together. If a loop happens to break, you just make another one! (Follow these instructions properly and that shouldn't ever happen.)

For a loop of 1 metre (40in) you will need:

- 10-15 grams of *rocaille* embroidery beads – you will be able to use the packets of tiny beads in the Workstation kit, or 10-15 grams of your own choice.
- 2.5 metres (100in) of strong nylon thread size 60, doubled, threaded with a beading needle.

PREPARATION Keep your stocks of beads in separate containers for the different colours. Make sure there are no small children or playful kittens in the room, and that the tiny beads cannot fall on to shaggy rugs or deep pile carpet!

METHOD First make a slip knot (see page 12) with both the ends of the doubled thread together.

Various bead sequence patterns are illustrated and you can thread in a random order. When you have reached the desired length, make sure you have at least 15cm (6in) at either end of clear doubled thread for getting a grip to tie the finishing knot.

Pull the tail to release the slip knot where you started; cut the other end to remove the needle.

Now hold all four strands in a bunch together and tie them in an overhand knot (page 13), tightening it by pulling the strands, in two bunches of two, away from each other quite hard. The knot should be smaller than a bead. Cut the ends close, and if you have used the recommended thread you can singe the whiskers to seal the knot. Otherwise the tiniest dab of light glue will hold it.

This long loop of love beads was made using the beads supplied in the kit. The diagram, above right, shows some bead sequence pattern ideas.

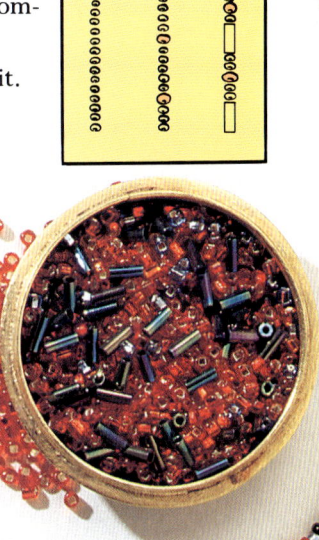

· Ideas For Beginners ·

Making Simple Earrings with Beads on Wire

The very simplest and quickest bead jewellery you can make is straightforward earrings of beads on wire.

Pick some interesting beads in pairs, perhaps to match a necklace or bracelet you are making. In the Workstation kit you will find the beads used for this elegant pair, and in a few minutes you could give yourself the finishing touch for day or evening wear.

As well as the beads, you will need:

- **A pair of earring hooks.** You can use the hook wires included in the kit, or you may prefer one of the other styles for pierced or non-pierced ears, as shown on page 11.
- **A pair of filigree cups.** You can use the ones supplied in the kit.
- **Earring wires:** either a pair of eyepins or headpins. Eyepins are also included in the kit and will help you get started, though as you get more experienced you may prefer to use jeweller's wire to cut and shape your own lengths as required.
- **Round-nosed jeweller's pliers.**

METHOD If using the eyepins you only have to thread your beads on to the wires with the loop at the bottom, then bend a second loop at the top of each wire which will be linked to the loop of the earring hook. Take care to bend the loop around the nose of the pliers to make a good shape, and give the wire a small bend backwards in the opposite direction so that it resembles the preformed loop and is properly centred, then bend it shut. When working using wire you will also need to form the loop at the bottom before you start.

Extra dangling drops can hang below the main earring by linking on to the bottom loop. Make sure you bend each wire loop closed.

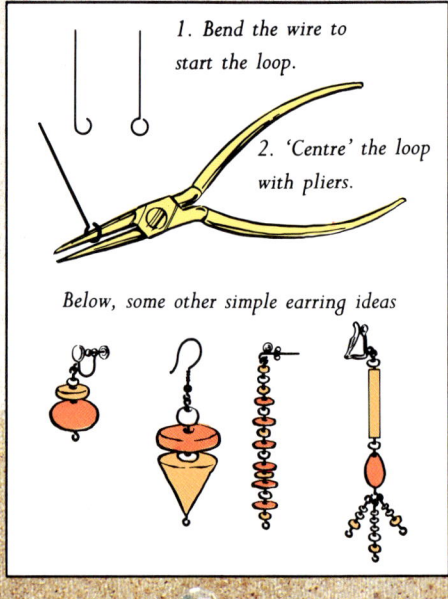

1. Bend the wire to start the loop.

2. 'Centre' the loop with pliers.

Below, some other simple earring ideas

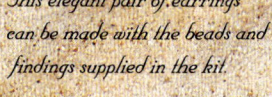

This elegant pair of earrings can be made with the beads and findings supplied in the kit.

· Ideas For Beginners ·

Worry Beads

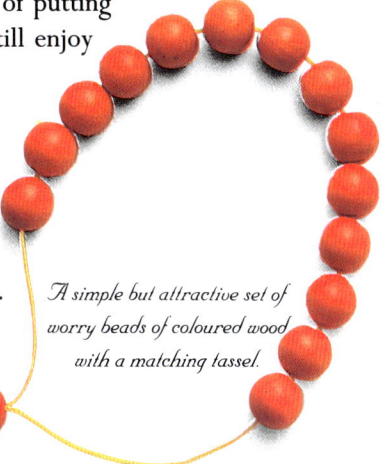

This may be the first introduction, for some people, to the pleasure of beads. Even if you are nervous of putting beads round your neck or wrist, you can still enjoy the feel of them as you relieve your stress!

The traditional Greek worry beads or 'Komboloi' are a short string of 15 beads loosely strung, ending with a tassel. It is thought they derive from the older prayer beads of many religions used as a memory aid in the repeated reciting of long prayers. The Christian Rosary, said to have been introduced by St. Dominic in the 12th

A simple but attractive set of worry beads of coloured wood with a matching tassel.

century has 150 beads, Muslim strings have either 33 or 99, and Hindu, Tibetan and Buddhist often have 108. If one bead is more important than the others, it will usually be the bottom bead, which has both ends of the cord through it and ends in the tassel.

Worry Beads used to be made of amber, horn, or black coral from the Persian Gulf. Nowadays metal, glass or plastic beads are quite acceptable.

You will need:

- **15 beads with smooth large holes. These are often called 'pony' beads.**
- **30 cm (12in) leather thonging, or silky cord.**

METHOD Thread all the beads on quite loosely, returning through the first bead as shown, with a knot or two knots below the bottom bead.

If you find it difficult to push the cord through, use a piece of sticky tape around the end to prevent the strands unravelling, which can then be removed afterwards. A matching tassel can also be made of any interesting silk or embroidery threads by following the diagrams.

How to make a tassel:

loop a length of thread and tie it at the top with a knot.

Wind some thread around the loops to make a tight bunch.

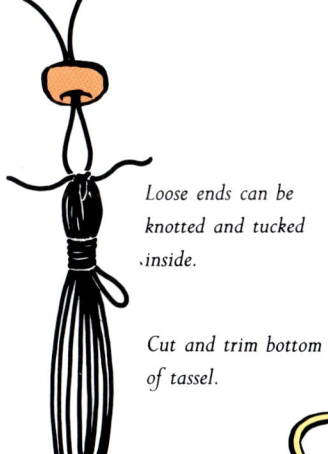

Loose ends can be knotted and tucked inside.

Cut and trim bottom of tassel.

Chokers

Choker necklaces are making another comeback in fashion to complement low necklines. They can be seen in many 18th century portraits and Edwardian ladies copied Queen Alexandra and then Queen Mary wearing broad chokers of pearls or jet to draw attention to swan-like necks or to conceal the sagging signs of ageing and scars from goitre surgery.

A choker is a tight-fitting necklace fastened close around the throat. It is sometimes a short single strand threaded as a normal necklace, but often a broad flat strip like a dog collar. They can be made in various ways:
- *as a velvet ribbon* with a decorative motif in the centre.
- *as a wide band* of three or more parallel rows of beads kept in shape with 'Spacer bars' pierced with a row of holes.
- *as a strip of beadwork,* worked with one needle and thread and *rocaille* beads into an openwork pattern.
- *as a strip* woven on a bead loom (see the chapter on beadweaving).

As neck sizes vary quite a lot, the most versatile fastening will be adjustable. The ends of a band of beadwork or beadweaving may be stitched securely on to velvet ribbons or strips of soft leather which can be tied, or a buckle can be stitched on with more than one position for closing, or velcro fastening can be used. If the strands are left long at each end, they can be plaited to make a solid cord for tying in a bow, as in the following project.

American Indian Style Choker

Since merchants began to trade with the natives of North America in the 16th century, European beads have been incorporated into the ornamentation of costume, and combined with beads of quill, shell and bone to make distinctive amulets and tribal jewellery. Wonderful authentic examples are on display in museums, and have been recreated in recent films.

To make this American Indian Style Choker, you will need:

- 4 metres (4 yards) of cord or thinnest leather.
- 12 bone hairpipe beads 5cm (2in).
- 27 pony beads. These are large-holed beads of glass or metal. For an authentic look, use silver and turquoise colour beads.

METHOD Follow the threading diagram as shown. Finish off the choker at each end with an overhand knot of all four strands together. Then plait them to a length of at least 15cm (6in), knot and trim the ends to a tassel. If the strands are very thin, add extra strands to the bunch before tying the first knot next to the bead pattern at each end. You can experiment with unusual braiding patterns, but many fine threads can always be plaited in a three-strand plait by dividing all the threads into three bunches, like hair.

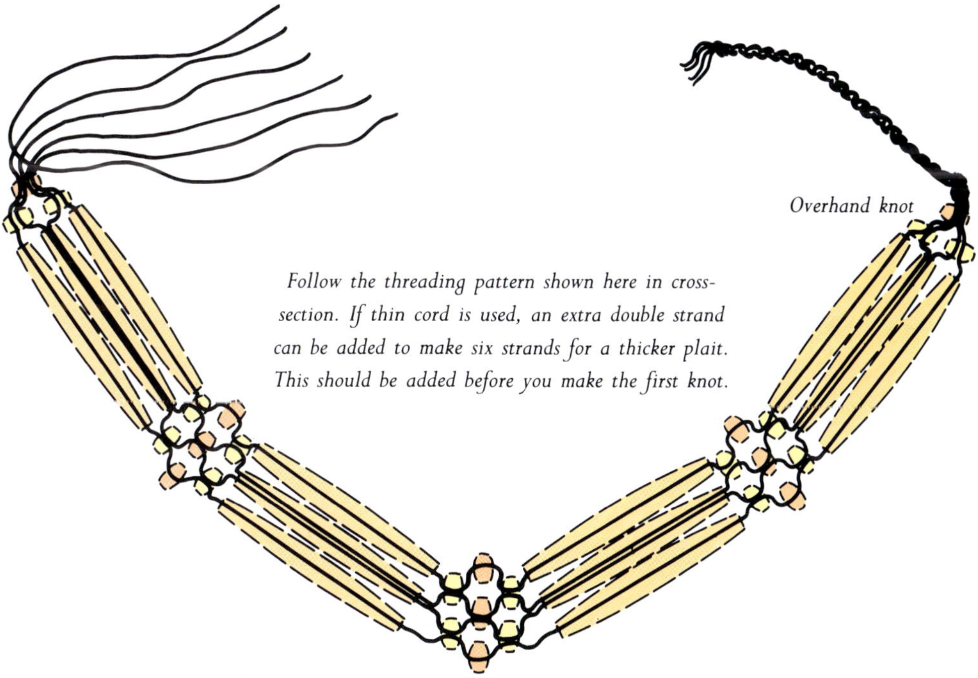

Overhand knot

Follow the threading pattern shown here in cross-section. If thin cord is used, an extra double strand can be added to make six strands for a thicker plait. This should be added before you make the first knot.

ELASTIC BRACELET

Of course, all the techniques for threaded necklaces can equally be used to make bracelets, or ankle bracelets. They have to be strongly made and if they do up, you have to bear in mind the need for a clasp that can be managed with one hand! However making a circular bracelet using elastic is extremely practical and needs no fastening, and if beads of wood, metal, glass or plastic with large holes are used, the patterns can be fun but not too complicated for a beginner to master. You can use colourful beads for a playful look, or grained wood for a gentle effect with natural tones. Two types of threading patterns are shown here, and as you progress through all the techniques, your experience with these will make the bead lace and some other beadwork patterns in later projects easier to understand. For both patterns, the quantities given are for a strip of approximately 18cm (7in) but you may wish to vary the length or use beads of a different size.

You will need:

PATTERN 1	PATTERN 2
• 52 wood or glass beads size 8mm.	• 56 wood or glass beads size 8mm.
• 1 metre round hat elastic in a single strand.	• 4 lengths of approximately 1/2 metre round hat elastic.

When threading is complete, make an overhand knot (see page 13). Do not pull the elastic too tight. Knots are less visible if they are positioned in the middle area rather than the edges of the work, and you may be able to pull the knot out of sight inside one of the beads. To complete pattern 2 you will need to tie 4 overhand knots.

Diagram for pattern 1, using a single strand of elastic.

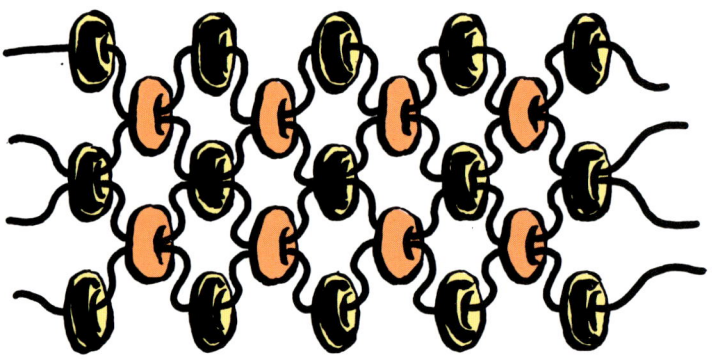

Diagram for pattern 2, using four strands of elastic.

• IDEAS FOR BEGINNERS •

The bracelet shown here follows pattern 1 and uses highly prized Venetian and Indian beads.

CHAPTER
• THREE •

ℬEADWORK

ℬeadwork jewellery is more complex than straightforward bead threading and can be more interesting to undertake. Beadwork employs a number of needlework techniques using 'rocailles' with thread to build up a piece. If you have a sufficient range of colours and enjoy patient and painstaking work, the most elaborate patterns can be created.

The work is undertaken with a fine needle and thread which goes through each bead at least once in a definite order building up a pattern. In bead lace techniques, one or more of the threads goes in and out, and only the beads hold the whole fabric together. With beadweaving, the warp is generally clear and only the weft thread travels through the beads. Bead embroidery can also be considered to be beadwork, although here the beads merely embellish an already existing fabric base.

As a home craft, beadwork is highly suitable, even if you live away from specialised suppliers. **Rocaille** beads are easily available by mail order, and with a stock of some good colours you will have the ingredients for a great many pieces of interesting work.

It is worth noting that a uniform size for small beads can be important in beadwork. As most suppliers' catalogues number the sizes differently, you may have to keep a sample with you when you are buying *rocailles* and bugles. Like knitting, patchwork or embroidery, once you have decided on a design you will have a very satisfying hobby.

In the UK, many beadwork techniques have been popular since Stuart times. Then, methods for producing tiny glass beads were sufficiently developed for quantity production, both in Venice and other parts of the world. Coloured glass beads were included on ornamental embroideries and were used to embellish clothing and jewellery. The beads made and used in Europe were also taken to the New World, where the natives incorporated them into the fine crafts they practised.

In the 18th and 19th centuries, the American Indians and native Africans further developed their own distinctive patterns and complex techniques. With horsehair or waxed linen thread, fine beads could be threaded; and as steel needles came to be made longer and thinner, beadwork techniques became ever more sophisticated and even smaller beads could be used.

The items of jewellery shown here are both antique pieces of bead weaving, worked with tiny beads on a loom.

Beadwork Daisy Chains

This is one of the simplest and most effective beadwork patterns, and a good one to start with. The earliest mention of it that I have found is in an instruction booklet of 1913.

If you can obtain a quantity of *rocaille* beads in two or three different colours, you will be able to create a variety of individual pieces. And in a pattern like this it doesn't even matter if the sizes of the beads don't exactly correspond. By varying the colours and spacing of the daisies, you can make unique patterned strands. You could use the *rocailles* from the kit to make a long loop to hang round your neck, or several smaller pieces of jewellery. Even if you never learned any other technique, you could fill a stall at a market or craft fair with daisy necklaces, and no two would be the same!

SINGLE DAISY PATTERN

For a short necklace you will need:

- 7 grams of the stem colour.
- 2 grams of the petal colour.
- 1 gram of the colour for the centres of the daisies.
- A long thread of 60 thickness nylon thread, doubled on a beading needle, with the ends in a temporary slip knot, as shown on page 12.

For a 40cm (16in) necklace you will also need a clasp, such as the bolt ring and split ring shown on page 11, and if desired two 5mm (1/4in) lengths of gimp, as more fully explained on page 36. Slightly more beads are needed for a longer strand, but the finishing is simpler.

METHOD Thread 6 stem beads, 5 petal beads, 1 centre bead and go back through 1st petal bead. Thread 3 more petal beads, then back through the 5th petal bead to complete the daisy, and continue from the beginning. You can vary the lengths of stem between the daisies for a naturalistic effect.

Basic daisy chain pattern. When working these patterns, keep pulling up the slack as you go.

FINISHING OFF To finish off as a loop, first make sure it is going to be long enough to go over the head without bursting (60cm or 24in) then simply gather together the two lots of two strands and tie an overhand knot as you did with the love beads, following the steps on page 13.

For a short necklace with a clasp with or without gimp, begin by threading 1 stem bead, then thread through one piece of gimp if you have it and one loop of the clasp. Go back through the first bead, making a knot around the centre thread, finished with an overhand knot (see page 13) using the two strands which have come round on opposite sides of the centre thread. Pull it tight enough to avoid any slack and continue making the pattern. When you reach the other end, after the last stem bead thread a second piece of gimp if required and go through the loop of the second half of the clasp. Now thread through the end bead, cut the thread to release the needle and knot as at the beginning. The result should be a neat ending, with a fastener and knots concealed between two beads.

DOUBLE DAISY

This pattern has no stem, but just a profusion of daisies one after another. To make a bracelet, you will need:

- **10 grams of *rocailles*, but the colours can be mixed.**
- **1 larger round or disc-shaped bead as a button fastening.**
- **Use a single 60 thread, as some beads will have three threads through.**

METHOD: For the bracelet, begin at one end with a loop of sufficient beads to fit tightly over the bead to be used as a button, on the diagram it is 10 beads. Go round through the loop a second time for strength, and then start the pattern, counting the last two beads of the buttonhole loop as beads 1 and 2 of the pattern. As you work, keep pulling up the slack thread as you go.

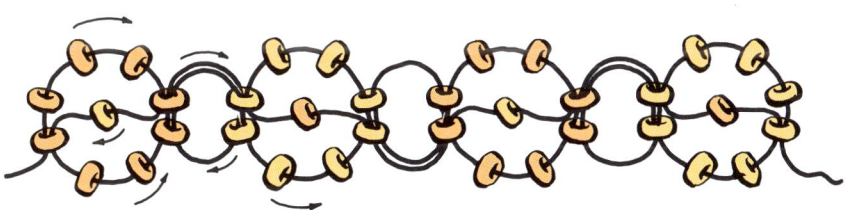

Double daisy pattern

Continue the pattern till the work is 18cm (7in) long, and finish with the addition of the button bead, securely attached as shown.

For starting and finishing knots, just tie an overhand knot in the end of the thread. If it is next to a bead with plenty of strands inside, then even if you pull, it should not slide out through the bead. If this is a problem, a tiny dot of light glue may be the answer, or a knot around one of the other threads.

Finishing a double daisy bracelet using a button bead.

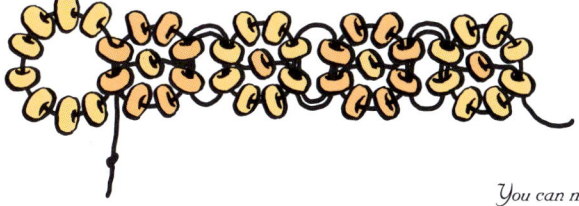
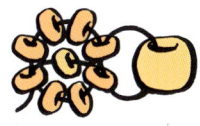

You can make a single daisy necklace as shown on the left or a double daisy bracelet (right), using the 'rocailles' supplied in the kit.

BEADWORK EARRINGS

The beauty of dangling earrings is that they frame the face, and because they hang free, their movement catches the light, adding an element of sparkle. Long beadwork earrings are very popular everywhere and though the basic construction is the same, by changing the patterns, the proportions, or varying the fringing at the bottom edge, an enormous range of designs can be produced, with dramatically different effects.

They are not only attractive but fun to design and make, and may be the work of just one or two evenings. These instructions explain one design, but you may prefer to try one of the others shown, or use the templates at the back of the book to design your own.

The structure starts with a solid row of parallel bugle beads threaded through from both ends which resembles a fence. Above this a solid triangle of beadwork in 'brick stitch' is built up, with a loop at the top that attaches to your earring hook. Below the row of bugles you can add an interesting fringe pattern, so that the earrings are full of movement when worn.

You will need:
- **10 grams of** *rocailles* **in the colours you have decided to use, and perhaps another 5 grams of bugles.**
- **Thread your beading needle with a single 60 thread. You will go through every bead at least twice so it must be strong and fine.**

METHOD For this pattern, thread 11 bugles, then return going through each from the other end as shown. Pull up all the slack as you work.

Then make the triangle at the top with *rocailles*, using brick stitch as shown. The needle goes down through each *rocaille* bead through the loop between the two bugle beads immediately below, and back up through the *rocaille* bead, then down again through the next *rocaille,* and so on. Each row decreases by one bead.

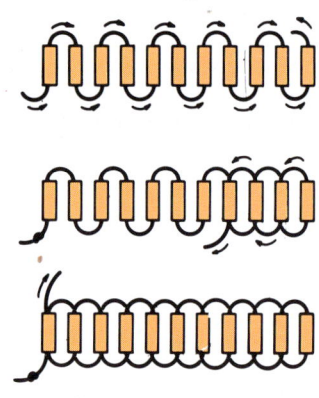

Above – making the initial solid row of bugles.

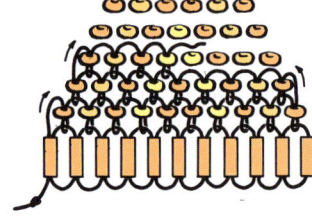

Above – 'brick stitch' is used to construct the triangle.

Left – **threading a loop at the top of the triangle.**

When the row of two beads is in place at the top, thread a sequence of eight *rocailles.* Go round through the complete loop a second time for strength before threading through the second bead in the top row, and take your needle in and out of one or two more beads before finishing off with a discreet knot around a thread. Go through another bead, do the same, pull tight, cut and finish off. ***Now for the fringe.*** If you can go through the bugles in the fence a third time with your thread, each strand of fringe can hang below each bugle. If there is no room for more thread inside the bugles, the fringe loops can be attached, like the brick stitch above, on to the loops of thread between the bugles.

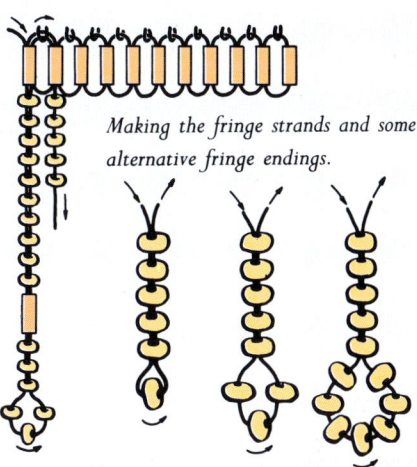

Making the fringe strands and some alternative fringe endings.

For each strand of the fringe, the needle and thread go down each sequence of beads through the bead at the bottom just once, turn round, and come back up through all but that one again. Then the thread attaches at the top through a bugle in the fence or on to one of the loops of thread, then down again to make the next strand of fringe.

The whole triangle pattern can be made only with bugles, or each 'brick' in the triangle can be composed of two or three *rocailles,* to build a much longer triangle.

Beadwork earrings are fun to design and make. The instructions on these pages are for the earring shown on the left which is made with 'rocailles', 'bugles' and hooks supplied in the kit.

· BEADWORK ·

The variety of designs for making beadwork earrings is almost endless. Here are a few possibilities which use more colours of *rocailles* and bugles.

Brightly coloured beads in a geometrical pattern with a tapering fringe.

A totally different effect is achieved using the colours randomly.

A 'rainbow' effect with a looped fringe with pointed ends.

Metallic bugles and coordinating 'rocailles' create a more sophisticated look.

Similar designs using loops but different patterns at the top.

Beadweaving Choker

Interest in Victorian needlework crafts and Native American Indian culture have given a boost to all kinds of beadwork, particularly beadweaving on a loom. Both women and men are happy nowadays to wear bracelets and neckbands or chokers which match the informality of T-shirts and jeans.

Real pieces of American Indian beadwork are rather rare and valuable. Most of the imported beadwork today comes from areas in South and East Africa or Asia, and similar techniques and patterns may originate in very different locations.

A little wooden bead loom, known as the 'Apache' bead loom, used to be easily available in many haberdashers and trimmings suppliers before the first world war, and needlecrafts publications of the time include patterns for all sorts of projects, from bracelets to muff chains. Today, bead looms of metal or wood can be found from the large bead suppliers, with rollers at each end to allow long lengths to be worked easily. The small beads for weaving need to be a uniform size even if you use several colours, so it's a good idea to buy them at the same time to make sure the sizes match. The *rocailles* used in beadweaving are shaped like fat miniature doughnuts. Designs are best worked out not on squared paper, but using the special grids printed at the back of this book. This pattern will make a narrow choker with a chevron motif.

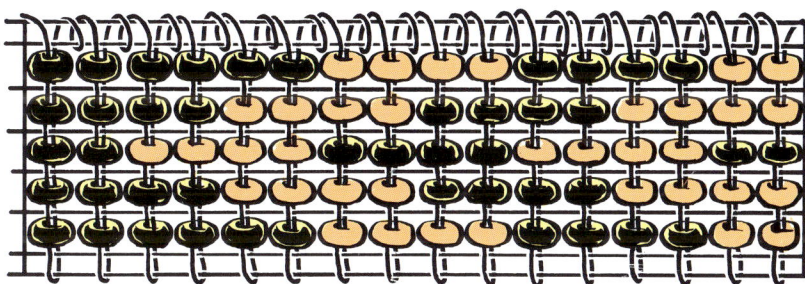

The 'chevron' motif, often used in beadweaving, can be worked in a variety of colours following the basic pattern shown here.

You will need :

* A bead loom.
* A size 12 beading needle.
* Three small packs of *rocailles* in harmonising colours (totalling about 15 grams) – you could use the beads in the kit with this workstation.
* Very strong fine thread, such as 60 nylon thread. If the colours are dark, use black thread.

PREPARATION Warp up your loom. Although the finished strip of weaving will only be about 31cm (12.5in) long, be generous with the warp threads as you need to allow a minimum of 20cm (8in) at each end of the woven strip in order to have enough to finish off properly.

The total warp length: at least 76cm (30in). This design is five beads wide, so the warp will consist of eight strands of 76cm (30in) as each edge needs two strands for strength.

Tie the bunch of warps together close to each end with an overhand knot. This can now be secured on to the nail on the roller at one end of the loom. Next, do the same at the other end, then tighten up the rollers, accommodating most of the extra length around one of the rollers. Now, position the warp threads parallel in the notches of the comb, first at one end, then in corresponding notches in the other. Remember that each edge consists of a double strand.

METHOD Start with a long thread in your needle. Shorter threads mean more frequent joining knots. The thread will be single, and if you pull it once or twice across a lump of beeswax it will be stronger and less likely to tangle.

To attach the weft thread, knot it around one of the middle warp threads and leave a tail of 20cm (8in), which will be plaited in with the warp ends when you finish off.

Weave the thread in and out like normal weaving for five rows. Try not to leave any slack as you go along. Now you are ready to start the beadweaving, which is done in a different way.

Hold the loom with the woven portion towards you. Start at the left edge, and work away from you. For the first two rows, work with one colour only to help establish the width. Pick up five black **rocailles** on your needle. Let them slide right down your thread next to the left hand edge. Pass the needle **under** the warps into your right hand. Use the left index finger to push up the row of beads from below so that each is held in its place between the warps.

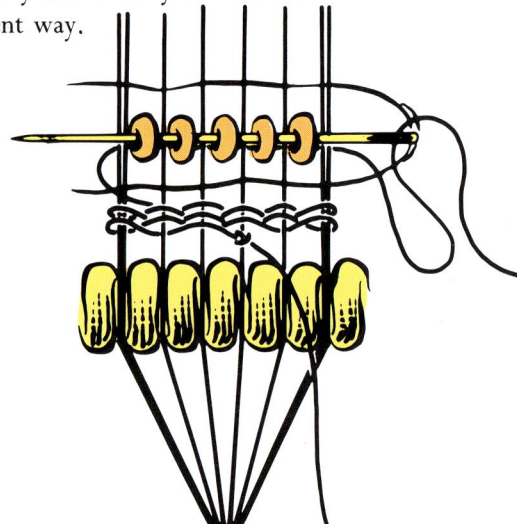

Beadweaving on a loom. *The left index finger is underneath the row of beads, pressing them up between the warps.*

Beadweaving choker made using the pattern shown on the previous page. The finished strip is shown with braided ends and strands ready to braid.

Taking the needle in your right hand, carefully push it back through each bead from right to left, *over* each of the warps.

Pull up the slack, firm but not too tight. This is your first row of beadweaving.

Repeat. (Every two or three rows it helps if you go around the left edge an extra turn which strengthens the whole weave.) Each pattern row is threaded up from left to right, but is only held securely in position by the return of the thread from right to left.

If you need to join a new weft thread, do not make the join at either edge where the knot will show. Instead, knot on the end of your new thread between beads in the middle of a left to right row, below the warp. Use a weaver's knot which has maximum grip and minimum bulk (shown on page 13). Leave 'tails' which can be trimmed off or stitched in out of sight later.

At the end of your strip, weave two final plain rows of beads as at the start, then five rows of thread woven in and out, finishing with a knot around one of the middle warps, leaving the tail of the thread dangling.

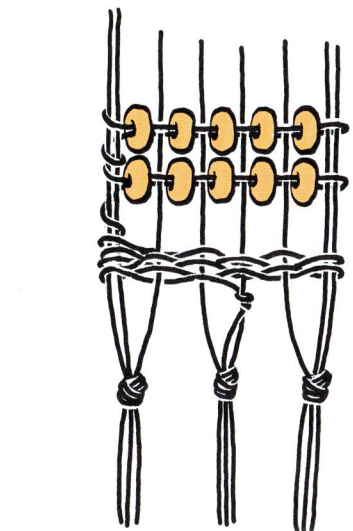

Finishing off. *Knot bunches of warps to prevent unravelling.*

To remove work from the loom, start with one end. After carefully disconnecting the warp and removing the strip from the row of notches, gather together the warp ends plus the end of the weft into three bunches of three and knot each together into an overhand knot. If you have used your own design on a wider warp, make sure the edges are knotted into bunches of three, the middle warps can be in pairs or threes. Repeat at the other end. Now the strip of weaving is secure and won't unravel, you can choose to stitch each of the strands back inside a row or two of the beads, or stitch the ends, or the whole thing on to velvet ribbon or soft leather, adding ties or Velcro.

CHAPTER
· FOUR ·

Making Beads

For anyone who lives far from bead suppliers and for the more adventurous designers among you, the commercial range of beads available just won't be enough. So break free – make your own!

Beads From Nature

One advantage if you live far away from shops is that you may be nearer to nature, the source of so many free raw materials.

We know beads were already being made long before humans had metal tools. Today, shells, seeds, nuts, twigs, dried flower heads, very small animal bones and feathers can all become jewellery ingredients with the help of a little imagination and some simple home tools such as a hacksaw, penknife and file, and perhaps a small drill.

Many small shells can be pierced with a darning needle if they don't already have a hole. You can easily push a needle through oak apples, and many pips, beans and seeds when they are fresh, as they harden only gradually. Try apple or melon pips, beech nuts, acorns and acorn cups. Olive or date stones will drill longways easily with a narrow drill after you have filed the ends flat.

The assorted jewellery shown here includes beads of nuts, shells and seeds. The acorn cup necklace, far right, is made by Carolyn Belson.

BEADS FROM JUNK

Other items that can be threaded include macaroni, polo mints, metal nuts and washers, old clock and watch parts, toy wheels, cut up drinking straws, tubing.

There is no restriction on recycling objects you find as beads and threadable components. Try corks, small sponges, buttons, cracker charms, fish vertebrae, defunct keys, tiny padlocks, small containers, whistles and bells, cotton reels and so on. Queen Victoria even had her children's milk teeth mounted on a necklace!

Necklace of crumpled sweet wrappers by Carolyn Belson.

PAPIER ROULÉ BEADS

Beads made of rolled paper have featured both in jewellery and in home decoration (bead curtains and lampshade fringes) since early this century.

You will need:

- **Old magazines with good quality paper and full page colour pictures, or giftwrap. Alternatively you can use sheets of good writing paper, either coloured or painted.**
- **Wallpaper paste (or white PVC glue that hardens transparent).**
- **Knitting needles or skewers.**
- **A ruler and good paper scissors (or a craft knife).**

METHOD At the back of this book you will find a page showing the most economical layout for cutting the strips from a rectangular page.

Once you have a pile of cut triangular strips, each one needs to be pasted carefully avoiding the first 15mm (3/4in) at the wide end to prevent sticking to the knitting needle. Then, starting at the wide end, roll the strip around the needle as shown. They should be left to dry thoroughly, and can be varnished to help make them last longer. The triangular shape makes a long narrow oval bead, similar to the bone ones used in the American Indian style choker on page 18.

Rolling up a paper bead.

Necklace of papier roulé beads made using strips from magazine pages.

Modelled Beads

As well as pottery and porcelain and the new modelling materials now on the market that harden by themselves or in a domestic oven, there are age-old recipes for fragrant beads of rose petal paste, flour, salt and water 'dough', or papier maché. Even sealing wax can be used either as complete blobs for beads or added to the outside of unvarnished plain wood beads, to give a relief design and colour.

The advantages of 'Fimo' and other synthetic polymer clays are the variety of colours, the relative simplicity of use and the capacity for keeping detail and not shrinking. You can obtain many colours which may be used together without any colour 'bleeding'. Beads can be made as spheres and then little round or long shapes of other colours can be pressed around the outside. Very sophisticated patterns can also be created, rather like a Battenberg cake or Swiss roll in a loaf form, then rolled or pulled out long and thin without losing the design which appears when the sausage is sliced. The cross-sections can be used as pattern units.

Illustrated here are modelled 'Fimo' bead jewellery made by Akiko Kase, with designs based on ancient Roman and Venetian glass patterns.

Making Beads

PREPARATION FOR WORKING WITH 'FIMO' When modelling, use a clean smooth working surface. You will also need a sharp blade or craft knife, and metal or wood skewers, not only for making the holes but to support the beads without touching them during firing. A skewer makes a hole large enough for leather thong or cord, while a darning needle-sized hole will only take a thinner thread, or wire if you are designing beads for earring making.

Before starting any modelling, knead the contents of each packet very thoroughly so that when it is folded, it will stretch rather than crack.

N.B. When you start working with 'Fimo', you must follow the manufacturer's safety instructions.

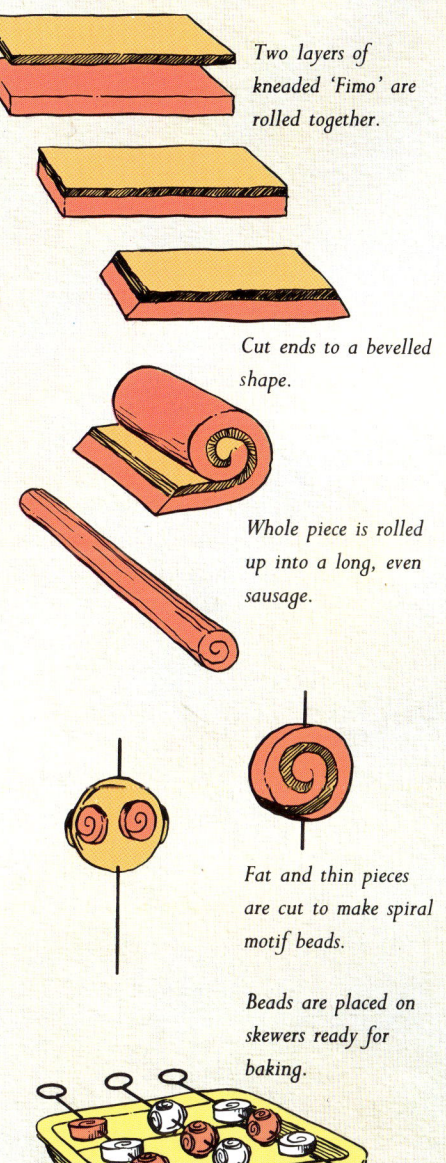

Two layers of kneaded 'Fimo' are rolled together.

Cut ends to a bevelled shape.

Whole piece is rolled up into a long, even sausage.

Fat and thin pieces are cut to make spiral motif beads.

Beads are placed on skewers ready for baking.

To make a Swiss roll spiral:

Roll out a layer of one colour into a rectangle (about 1/4 of a pack). Using a second colour, with about 1/8 of a pack, roll out a thinner rectangle of a similar size. Place one over the other, press together without trapping air between the layers. Roll flat and cut the edges to a neat rectangle, but not too thin. Save the trimmings which can be used to build up a bead underneath the surface where it won't be visible.

Using the craft knife, pare the two shorter edges to a wedge or bevelled shape, as shown. Now carefully roll it up into a spiral 'sausage'. Carefully roll with both hands on the table surface in front of you, until it is at least 20cm (8in) long. Cut about 2cm (1in) off each end (keeping the offcuts), and the spiral pattern should be visible but small. You can now cut fat little slices and pierce them edge to edge to make beads, or cut thin slices which can be pressed on to the surface of round beads in a repeating pattern. If you roll out the remainder again, you will have the same pattern in several sizes.

Arrange the skewers with the beads still on them on your baking tray or oven rack so that the outside surfaces are not touching anything. When they are 'done', you can usually pull them off their sticks before they cool.

I've found it very useful to have an oven thermometer that shows low temperatures to avoid any risk of burning or discoloration, or of never having the oven quite hot enough. In principle, longer baking is preferable to higher temperatures.

CHAPTER
• FIVE •

Professional Threading

Anybody can put a thread through a few beads, but now you are ready to practise the techniques for a professional finish. For design inspiration you have over 30,000 years of bead history to draw from, and if you notice what ordinary people around you like to wear, as well as following the top fashion magazines, you will never be short of ideas.

Straight Threading – the Classic Necklace

Follow this step-by-step method to thread the most basic single string of regular or graduated beads with a fastener at the back. You can do it whether you are rethreading a broken string or creating a new design using beautiful old or new beads. Do not attempt to thread with knots between the beads until you have mastered the principles of this basic straight method.

PREPARATION Choose all your beads with the same even-sized holes. Avoid using any beads with sharp edges inside as they will tend to cut the strongest thread. Beads can be laid out on a piece of velvet or corduroy on a tray, or if the sequence is intricate and there is a likelihood it may need to be moved before threading, try rolling out a flat thin layer of modelling clay (Plasticene) on the tray. Beads arranged and pressed into place won't roll about but can easily be picked up one at a time as required for threading.

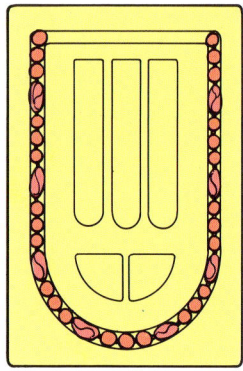

Beads in place on a beadboard ready for stringing.

Arranging beads on a bead board You should allow at least 2.5cm (1in) of the smallest beads either side of the fastener. This enables an easier grasp of both parts of the fastener and makes the necklace more comfortable to wear. Other beads are paired up on either side for symmetry. The centre bead should have the largest circumference.

Having decided on your bead arrangement, you will also need:

• **A doubled thread on a home-made needle of fuse wire as shown on page 10.** For this type of threading technique, the needle is made of about 10cm (4in) of the thinnest fuse wire (3 or 5 amp) which is folded double and the ends twisted together. The thread should be 40 nylon yarn if you can get it. It needs

to be at least 30cm (12in) longer than the estimated length of the finished necklace. *Do not try this method with 'Fishing line' (nylon monofilament or gut).*
• **Bolt ring fastener and split ring.** These are good to learn with, although any fastener with loops would be equally good, and you may prefer the look of a more ornate clasp.
• **2 pieces of Gimp,** cut not more than 1cm (3/8in) long, and of the same colour as the clasp.

METHOD Follow the steps below to thread your sequence.

1 Secure the doubled end of the thread with a slip knot, leaving yourself at least 30cm (12in) extra length. Then thread the first bead, followed by the gimp and bolt ring.

2 Take the thread back through the first bead, followed by all the other beads in the sequence. Add the second piece of gimp and then the split ring. Push the sequence down a little to give yourself some clearance, and remove the wire needle by untwisting it. Do not cut any thread at this stage.

3 Reach *in* through the end loop with finger and thumb (a). Grasp the split ring plus gimp (b) and move them *out* through the loop (c), placing both sides of the loop together as shown.

4 Slide the gimp back along the doubled thread as shown until it can't go any further.

5 Now gently tighten up the loop like a noose, by holding on to the fastener and pulling the length of thread holding the beads away from it.

6 Now the sequence of beads can be slid back towards this finished end. Release the slip knot and pull the threads carefully through to take out all the slack without letting the gimp slide out of sight inside the end bead.

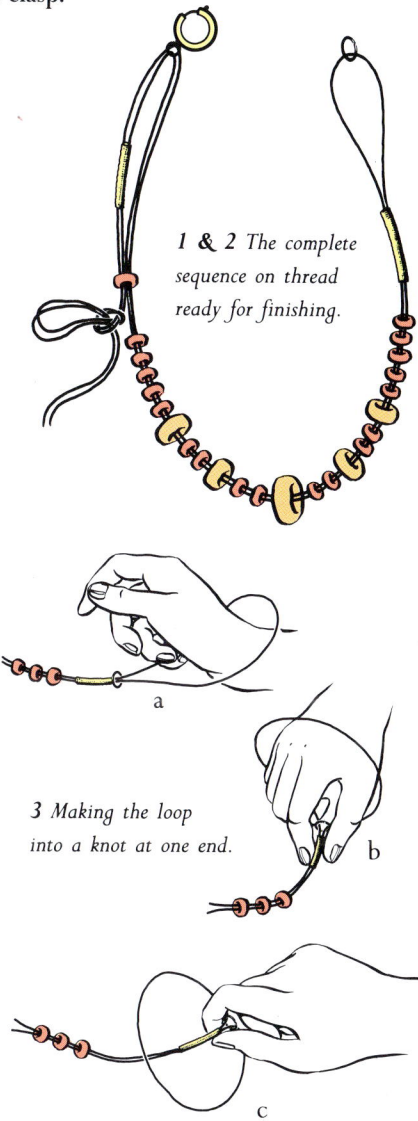

1 & 2 The complete sequence on thread ready for finishing.

3 Making the loop into a knot at one end.

4 Slide the gimp as far as it will go in the direction of the arrow.

5 This end is now pulled tight.

6 Release the slip knot and pull to take out the slack.

To finish off the whole necklace
After an extra pull to eliminate any possible slack, tie a half hitch knot as shown with the two ends around the centre thread, between the end bead and the next one. By pulling hard with the ends now, you will be able to make the whole necklace taut. Divide the two ends of the tail, keeping a good grip on both, and bring them around the centre thread again, in opposite directions (a, b). Holding the two strands together as one, tie them in an overhand knot and tighten by pulling them away from each other (c).

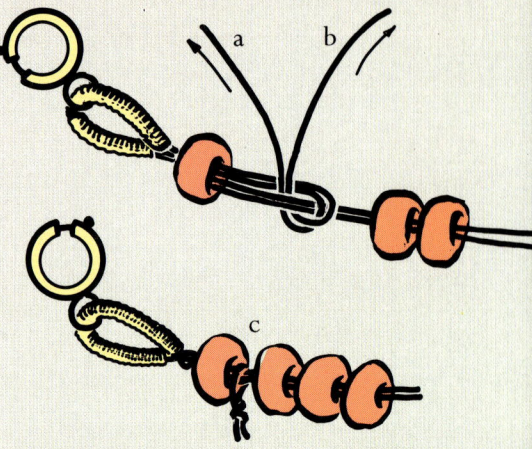

Tying a half hitch knot and finishing with an overhead knot.

If you have used the recommended nylon thread you can pull quite hard and the thread won't break. Even if the necklace seems rather stiff, in a short time it will relax and hang properly without being loose.

When you are quite satisfied with your knot, cut the ends close, and if it is nylon thread you can singe the ends with a match to seal and prevent unravelling, as described on page 13. This is the only knot on the whole necklace, and should be barely noticeable. (When some other thread is used, you will probably have to pull the ends inside the second bead along with the smallest drop of light glue, not superglue.)

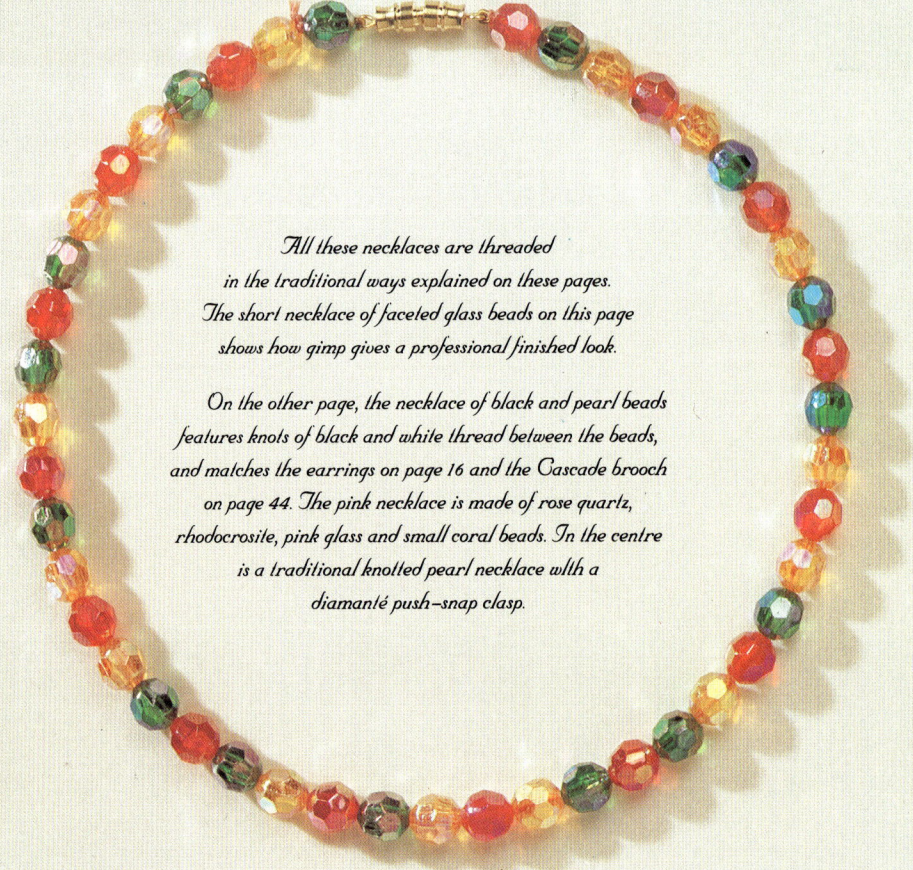

All these necklaces are threaded in the traditional ways explained on these pages. The short necklace of faceted glass beads on this page shows how gimp gives a professional finished look.

On the other page, the necklace of black and pearl beads features knots of black and white thread between the beads, and matches the earrings on page 16 and the Cascade brooch on page 44. The pink necklace is made of rose quartz, rhodocrosite, pink glass and small coral beads. In the centre is a traditional knotted pearl necklace with a diamanté push-snap clasp.

Professional Threading

Pearl Knotting

Once you are feeling really confident with the skills involved in the straight necklace, you are ready to tackle more advanced threading. Do not attempt to do this project without having mastered the techniques described in the previous pages.

Knotting between beads not only protects the beads, but makes a necklace slightly longer and adds to its beauty. In former times, silk was always used for pearls and precious beads, and as the craftsmanship was cheap, it didn't have to last because the pearls would be rethreaded every year.

Nowadays our advanced threads last much longer and we can make the job just as beautiful. The spun nylon thread comes in a selection of good colours in '40' thickness, and a necklace can combine two colours to make an interesting harmony with the beads used. Knotting will only be useful if all the beads used have the same size holes, and thread to be used should be as thick as will fit. For the beads in this project the thread used is composed of four strands, a doubled white and a doubled black, on the fuse wire needle as used in the previous project. For a short 46cm (18in) necklace, your **doubled** thread length will need to be at least 130cm (50in) to allow ample space for the knots.

You will need:

- **130cm (100in) of black, and the same of white 40 nylon thread.**
- **Two pieces of thick gimp 1cm (3/8in) long, and matching colour clasp.**
- **Beads laid out ready on your bead board. Allow an additional 1cm (3/8in) for every 10 knots when estimating the total length of the finished necklace, and 1.5cm (3/4in) for the length taken up by this 7mm bolt ring clasp and the finishing loops covered with gimp. Again a more elaborate single strand clasp could be chosen.**

METHOD Start with a slip knot in the end of the thread as before, and thread the first bead, the first piece of gimp, the bolt ring, then back through the first bead, taking care not to scrunch up the wire needle, tangle the thread or damage the gimp!

Now, just thread the entire sequence of beads on to your thread and finally your second piece of gimp and the split ring. Push everything a short way down the thread so you can work the end. Remove the wire needle by untwisting as before, but do not cut any thread.

Take extra care if you are using four strands. As in the straight threading necklace, reach **in** through the end loop with finger and thumb, grasp the ring plus the gimp and move them **out** through the loop (step 3, page 37). Place both sides of the loop together. Slide the gimp carefully along until it can't go any further. Now you can tighten the noose, and the ring should be securely held at the end with a circle of thread covered in gimp.

Before you make the first knot, slide the first bead that follows at this end up against the gimp. There will not be any knots next to the clasp at either end. The first knot is made **between** the first and second beads.

The knot used is a simple overhand knot. Do not attempt to tie this as a double knot of any kind, as not only will it become impossible to tighten in the place where you need it, but it always ends up looking scruffy! Work on a surface, not in mid-air, as bits that dangle will pull and tangle. Make the knot loosely, and then move it as close as you can to the first bead before allowing it to tighten. Some pearl stringers find that a darning needle through the loop of the knot will help. If you are using nylon thread you can now finish tightening the knot by pulling the two strands of thread (or two lots of two if the thread has four strands) away from each other quite firmly.

Slide the second bead along right up against the first knot. Make the next knot in the same way. Continue until every bead is held by a knot, up to the *third* from the end as shown.

Slide down the second bead. Release the temporary knot and pull everything through to eliminate any slack, taking care that the gimp hasn't disappeared inside a bead.

Tightening the knot using a darning needle through the loop and pulling the strands to tighten.

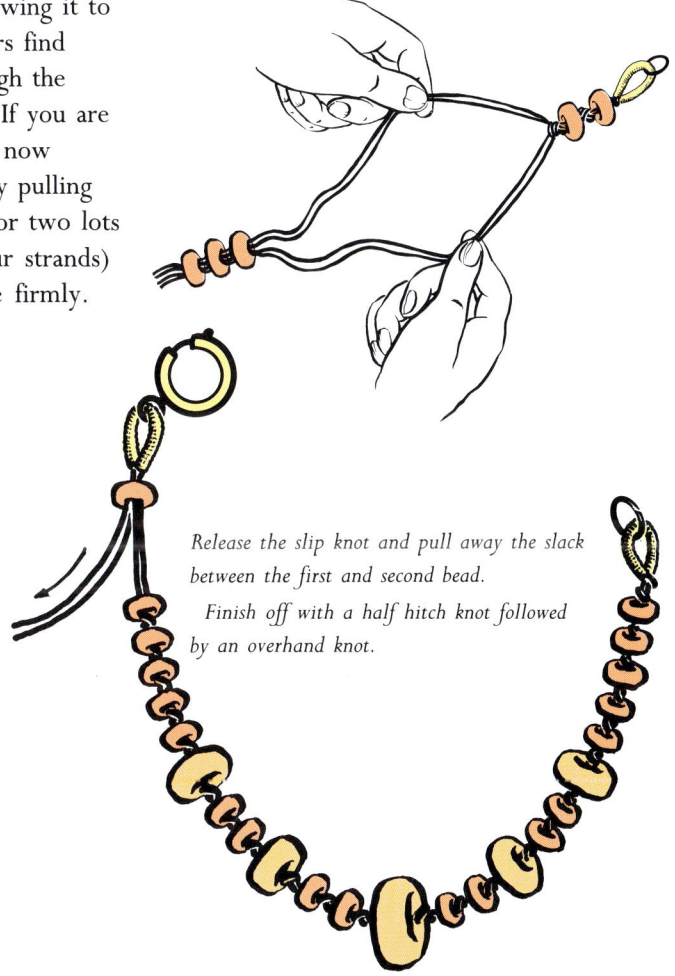

Release the slip knot and pull away the slack between the first and second bead.

Finish off with a half hitch knot followed by an overhand knot.

The final knot will be tied in exactly the same way as on the straight threading necklace. Tie a half hitch knot with all the end strands around in the space between the two final beads, pull the knot tight, then divide the strands into two bunches of two. Take them around the centre in opposite directions, fixing them together where they meet on the other side with a final overhand knot pulled very tight, before cutting the ends close and singeing with a match to seal the final knot.

If the finished necklace feels a bit stiff, this means you have done a very good job, as the knots tend to relax in use.

When threading pearls, you may prefer not to risk bringing a match anywhere near the work. You can seal the last knot with a tiny drop of light glue or nail varnish.

CHAPTER
· SIX ·

Further Ideas

Now you have sampled many of the techniques and are probably impatient to get to work. Hopefully you will begin to have the confidence to make up your own designs. These additional projects offer just a few more possibilities for your inspiration.

Multistrand Necklace and 'Bunch' Earrings

A matching ensemble of jewellery including an elaborate necklace and earrings, bracelets or a brooch is called a *parure*.

This popular style of necklace is short but not tight, and can be worn with an open neck blouse or dress. With a rich profusion of tiny beads, it will accent your outfit by picking up colours from the clothes you are wearing. And together with the earrings it will create an impression of movement and sparkle close to the interesting part of you, your face!

For the whole set you will need:

- 120- 150 grams *rocailles* in toning colours.
- Beading needle threaded with doubled 60 thread.
- Necklace clasp, 1 pair earring hooks, 2 pairs bead cups, 2 pairs eyepins.

METHOD The necklace is approximately 54-60cm (21-24in). You will need to thread 12 loops of 115cm (45in), either keeping some strands to certain colours only, or all random sequences of the colour mix you have chosen. If the beads vary slightly in size, it adds to the texture and interest, and you can use up odds and ends of *rocailles* from other projects. At the end of threading each loop, make an overhand knot with the four strands together, tighten the knot and finish off securely in exactly the same way as you did when you threaded the love beads in the very first project, on page 15. Now make 11 more loops in the same way.

To assemble the necklace: Use your round-nosed pliers to open the loop of one of the eyepins, and bend it into a slightly larger ring. Collect all the loops of beads together in it, locating the joining knots close to the wire, then close it. Now push the wire through one of the cup shapes, bend the protruding end round, through one half of the clasp, and push the end back into the hole in the cup. Repeat at the other end of the necklace. You need not be too fussy about evening up the lengths of the strands of beads, as the necklace should hang with some shorter and some longer strands.

Further Ideas

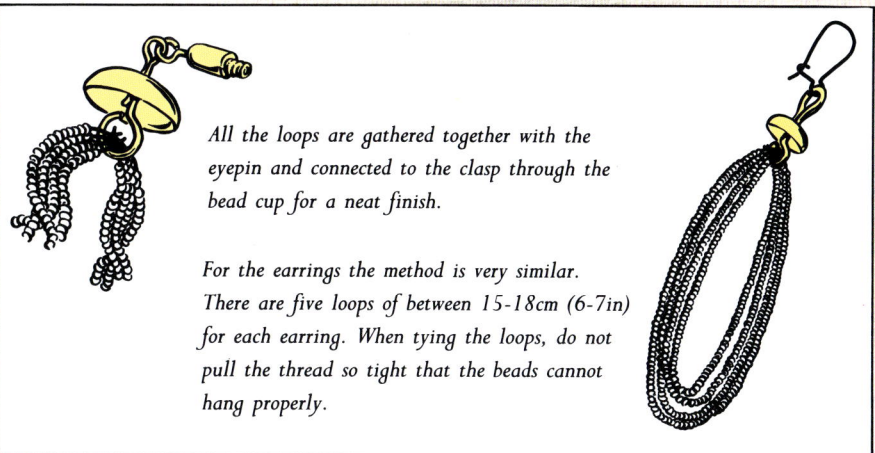

All the loops are gathered together with the eyepin and connected to the clasp through the bead cup for a neat finish.

For the earrings the method is very similar. There are five loops of between 15-18cm (6-7in) for each earring. When tying the loops, do not pull the thread so tight that the beads cannot hang properly.

A profusion of tiny twinkling coloured beads gives a luxurious look to this matching set of multistrand necklace and earrings.

Cascade Brooch

·Further Ideas·

Another jewellery accessory made with beads is this stunningly effective brooch, which will match the earrings on wire from page 16. It will look good on a lapel or floppy hat, or pinned on a piece of velvet ribbon worn around the throat.

Fittings can be obtained for making brooches using beads. A disc or oval-shaped template of metal, pierced with a network of tiny holes like a tea-strainer, can be completely covered with sparkly beads which can also cascade downwards. They are attached with fine wire and thread looped through the holes and secured at the back. Then the whole template clips on to a special matching brooch back, which conceals all the untidy wire ends and knots.

You will need:

- Template and brooch back.
- Soft wire such as florist's wire, or medium fuse wire.
- About 14 black 8mm beads.
- About 14 iridescent 6mm beads.
- About 10 faceted black 5mm beads.
- 5 grams silvery *rocailles* and a few black ones.

METHOD *Make the outer ring first.* Twist the wire ends together so that hardly any gap shows. Make the second ring with a separate wire and adjust the exact size to fit within the first. Do the same with the inner ring. The outer ring may be larger than the template but can still be attached to the edges. The wire ends can be used to fasten each ring in turn in one place on to the template, but they will need securing in three or four other places each. Use a short length of wire for each fixing, even if the back of the template looks like a tangle of twisted ends, it will all be covered with the back plate.

For elegant evenings, this brooch coordinates with the earrings you made on page 16.

·Further Ideas·

Building up the rings of beads, starting from the outer ring. Once all three rings are threaded, the cascade strands are added as shown.

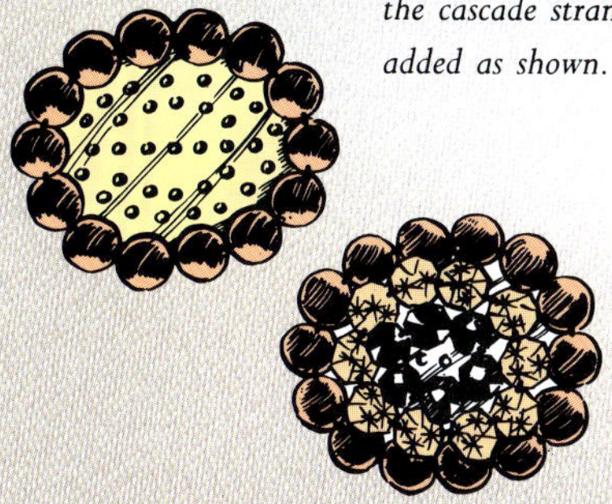

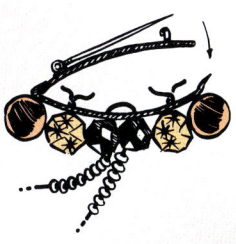

Putting the back on. This will cover all the spare wire ends.

For the cascade: Start at the back of the template. With a needle and thread, go through one of the centre holes, thread ten *rocailles,* a faceted black, five *rocailles* and one small black one, one iridescent one, another small black. Then go back up through the iridescent and all the others and back through the template. Emerge through a nearby hole and repeat, five times. Take care to use different holes, and knot the end of the thread to the tail that was left when you started. Using wire cutters, cut off as much of the spare wire ends as you can. Now fix on to the backing by bending the small lugs around the edges of the back, and press them down as smoothly as you can.

Earring clips with matching templates can also be made in this style.

The techniques for making the knotted necklace shown here in close-up are described in detail on pages 40–41.

Further Ideas

Beadwork Lace Collar

This is another basic beadwork pattern so popular that you will find adaptations of it all over the world, from Europe to Southern Africa, Greenland, Pakistan, Mexico and Indonesia.

The ancient Egyptians wore broad collars of wonderful tiny ceramic beads, and made beadwork pieces to include when they mummified their royalty, which were versions of the same open latticework stitch.

The pattern shown here is made as a strip with one needle and doubled 60 thread and can be made to any length you need. To make it into a curved collar, a second needle with doubled thread goes along the top edge, adding three extra beads between each top bead of the pattern that it goes through. This is the strand that is going to take any strain. It is not difficult to see how the lattice pattern could be elaborated for many interesting effects.

Among the Zulu women beadworkers, where clasps are scarce, they make an ingenious fastening with a clothing button or wider bead at one end, and a bead loop at the other end as a buttonhole. Instructions for this technique can be found with the double daisy bracelet, on page 25.

You will need:

- **Beading needle and 60 thread.**
- **30 grams of *rocailles* of the main colour (pearly white).**
- **5 grams of *rocailles* in a second colour for the connecting beads (mauve).**
- **Larger bead for a button if required, otherwise a clasp of your choice.**

METHOD Using a doubled 60 thread in your beading needle, thread two white **rocailles,** one mauve, then repeat the following sequence until the work measures approximately 50cm (20in).

- **three white** • **second mauve** • **three white** • **third mauve** • **three white** • **fourth mauve** • **three white** • **then back through fourth mauve** • **three white** • **fifth mauve** • **three white** • **sixth mauve** • **three white** • **back through sixth mauve**

To make it into a curved collar shape: The second doubled 60 thread goes through the first white bead. Add three white, then go through the white bead at the top of each loop in turn, with three white beads between each.

When this pattern threading is complete you should end up with all four strands emerging from the same white bead at each end. Now attach the fastener of your choice, or a button at one end and a beaded loop at the other.

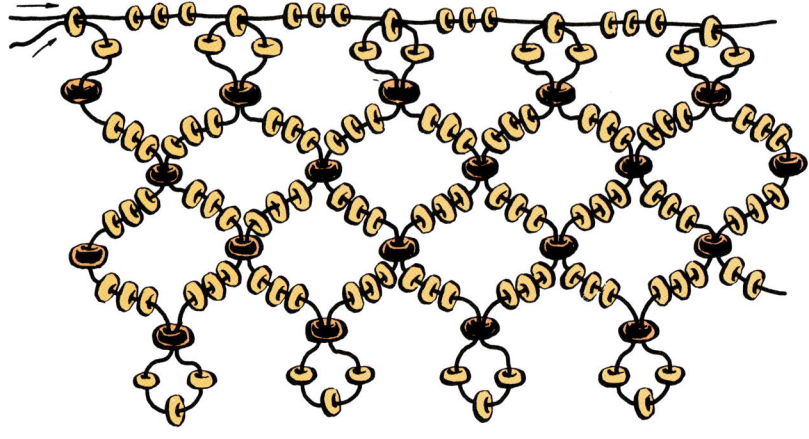

The Victorian look of this bead-lace collar makes it a charming idea for a bridesmaid.

ACKNOWLEDGEMENTS

All these people helped me in a variety of ways – getting me started with a word processor, advice and consultation over the threading instructions, lending examples, and all-round encouragement; Tom and Miriam Heatherwick, Marion Bloch, Carole Morris, Carolyn Belson, Akiko Kase, Maja Dezman and my mother Elisabeth Tomalin.

TO FIND SUPPLIERS

The Bead Society of Great Britain has a wide and lively membership with regular meetings, workshops, talks and an annual bead bazaar. All the important mail order suppliers are members and advertise regularly in the newsletter, which also features up-to-date news of exhibitions, tips for designers, reviews of new books and accounts of bead-buying expeditions and research in all corners of the world.

Send SAE for details to the Membership Secretary, Dr. Carole Morris, 1 Casburn Lane, Burwell, Cambridgeshire, CB5 OED.

This knotted gemstone necklace includes leopard skin, jasper, aquamarine chips and faceted smoky quartz beads.

The author's shop is called 'BEADS!' and is at 259 Portobello Road, London W11 1LR. There is no mail order or wholesale service available, only rare, antique, hand-made, one-off and collectable beads; also repairs and tuition.

In the US, the magazine **'Ornament'** carries addresses of regional bead societies and research organisations, together with all the big US mail order companies. Address for subscription enquiries: Ornament, PO Box 2349, San Marcos, CA 92079, USA.

As a matter of courtesy and to ensure a speedy reply always include an SAE or international reply coupon with any postal enquiries.

·Beadwork Earring Templates·

The following pages contain templates for designing beadwork earrings, necklaces and bracelets and grids for planning beadweaving designs.
The last 3 pages are for making papier roulé beads. The first layout is a guide for cutting strips from magazines and the last two can be coloured, cut and rolled into paper beads.

·Beadwork Earring Templates·

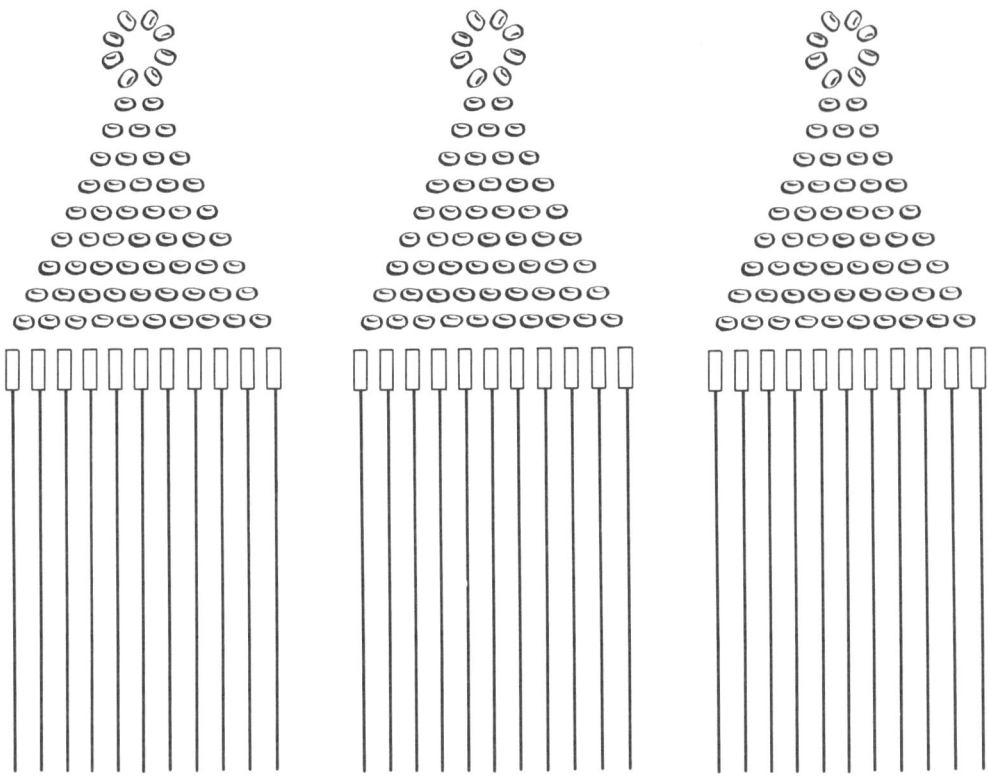

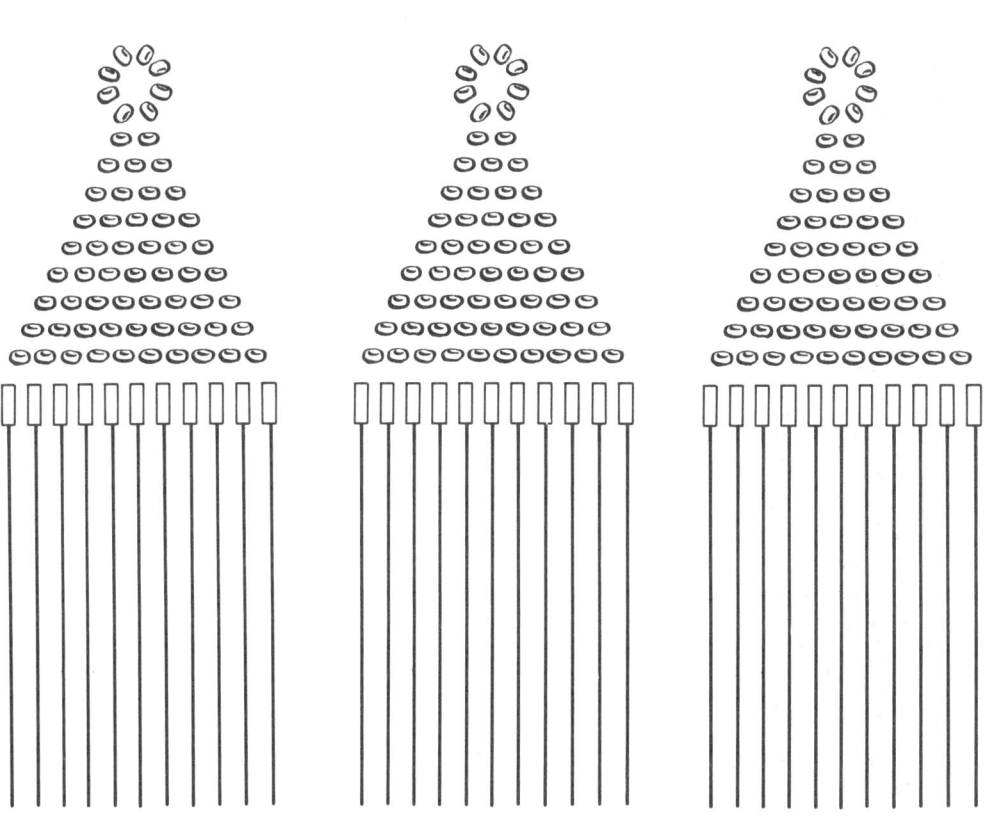

Necklace & Bracelet Templates

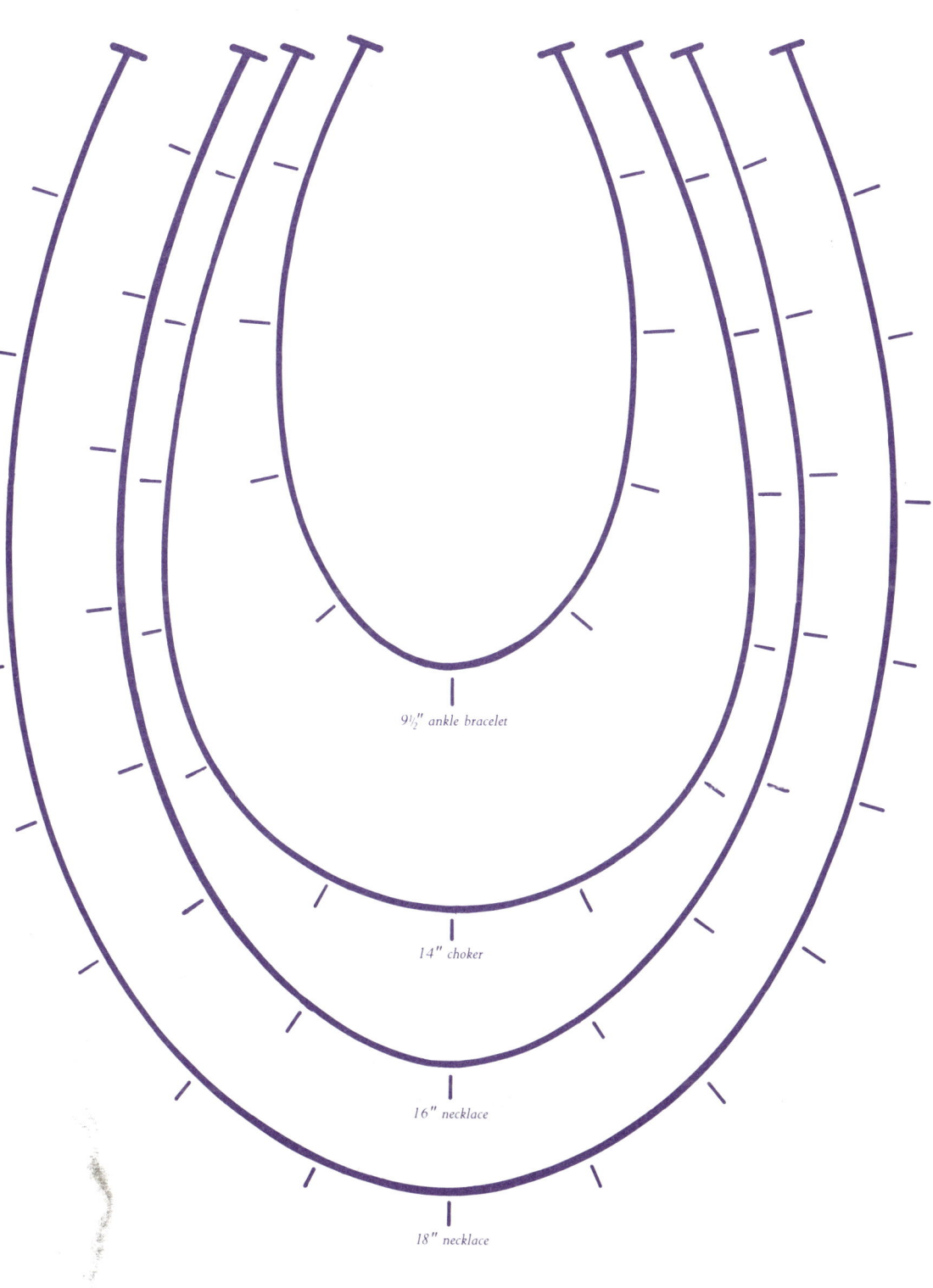

Necklace & Bracelet Templates

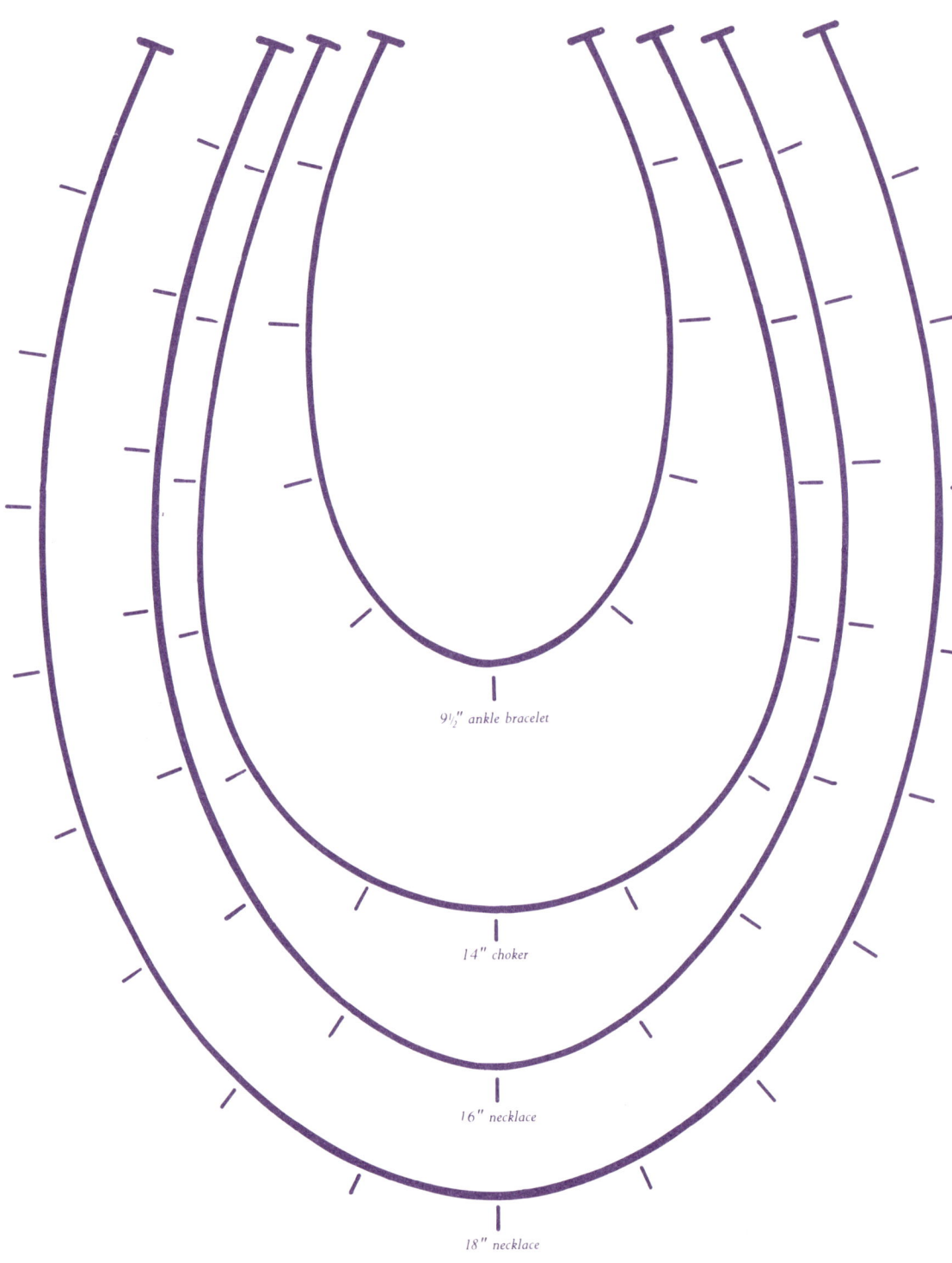

9½" ankle bracelet

14" choker

16" necklace

18" necklace

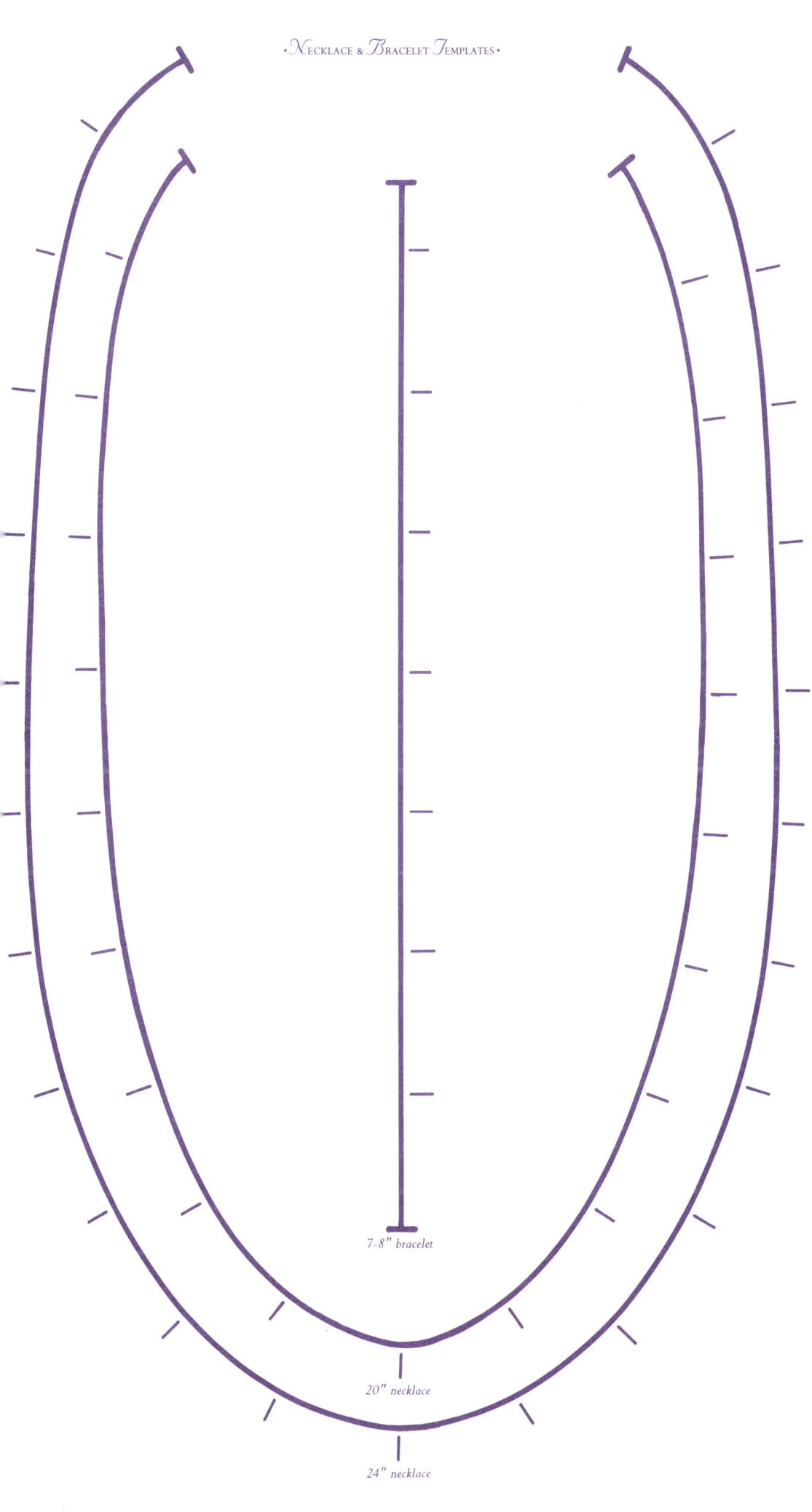

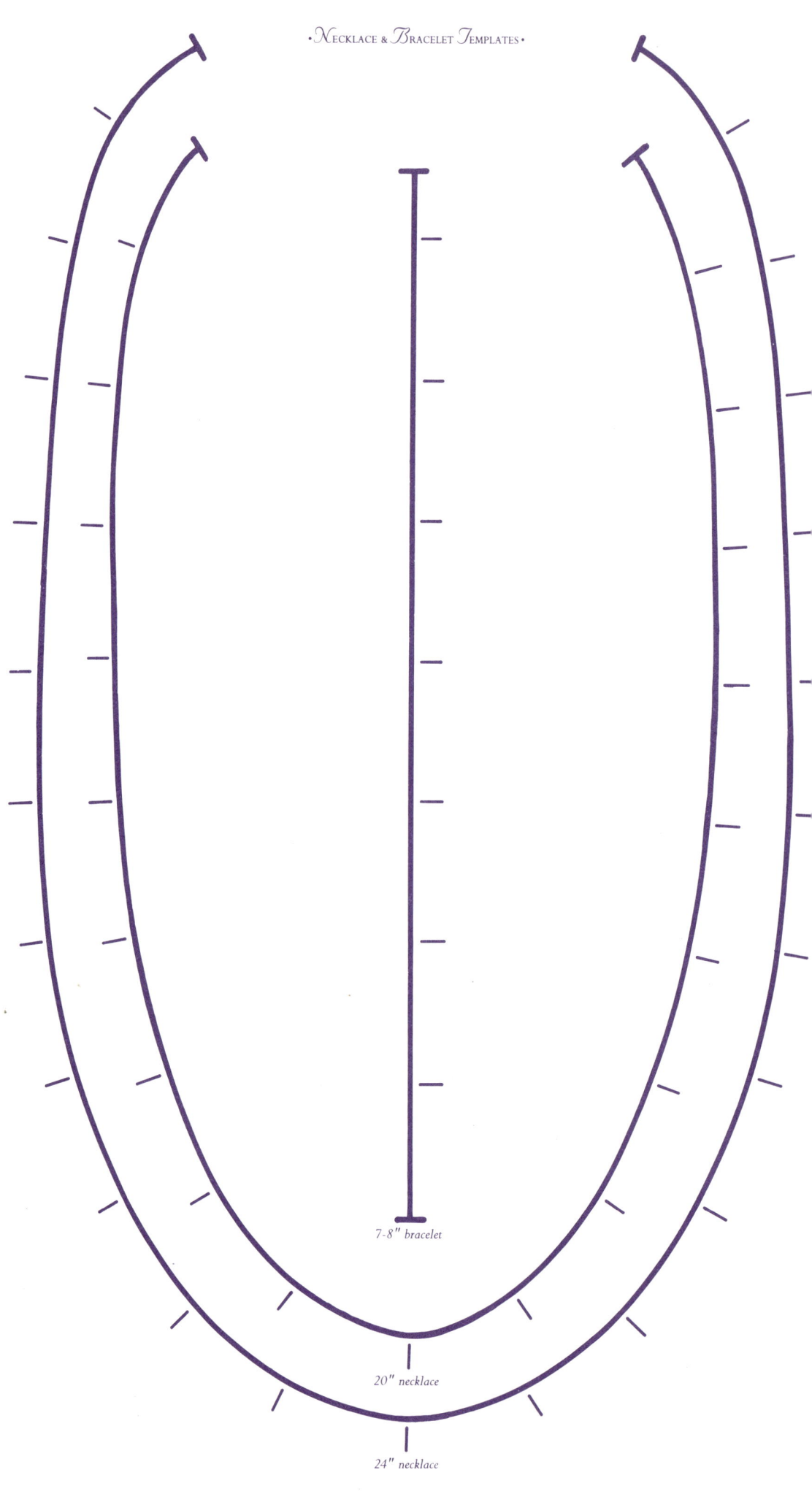

· Beadweaving Grids ·

Weft direction

Warp direction

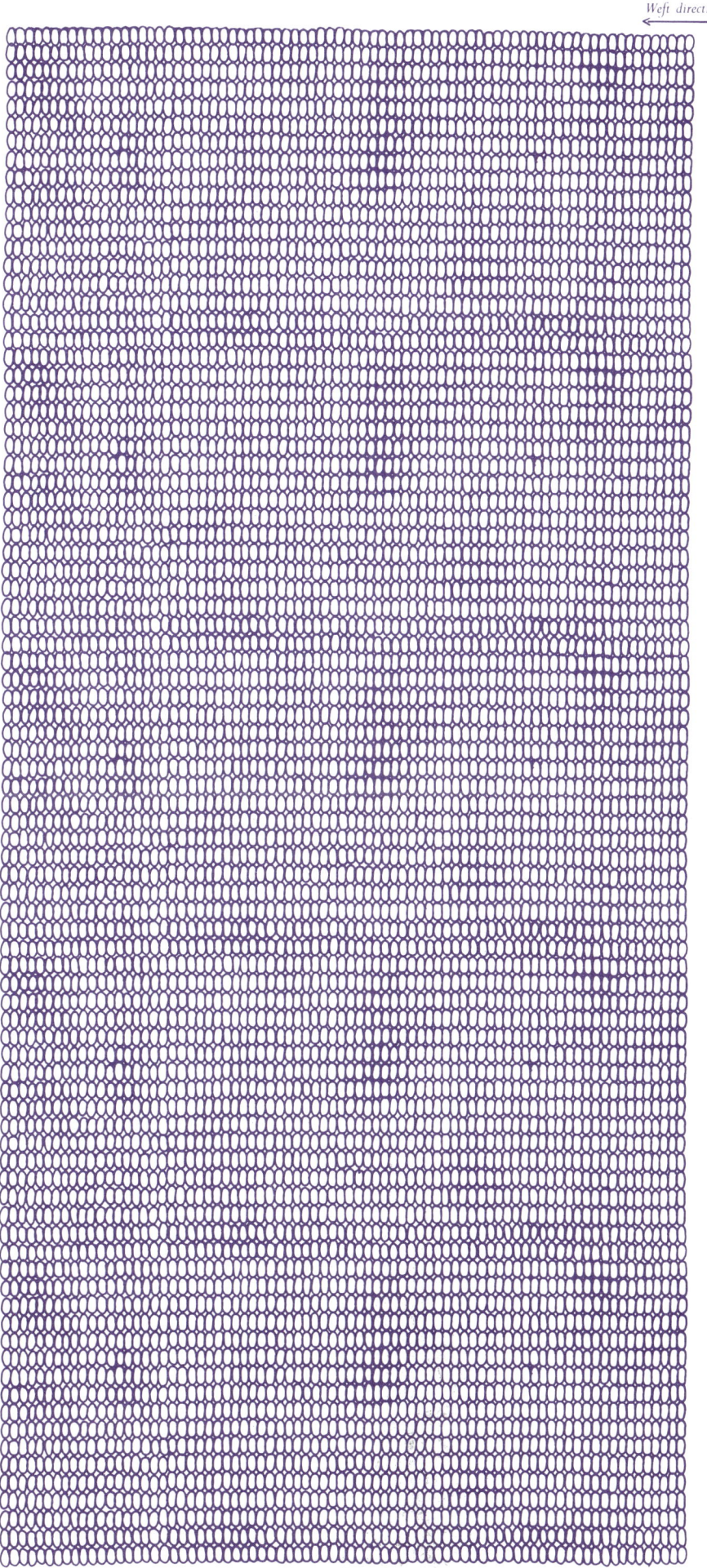

Beadweaving Grids

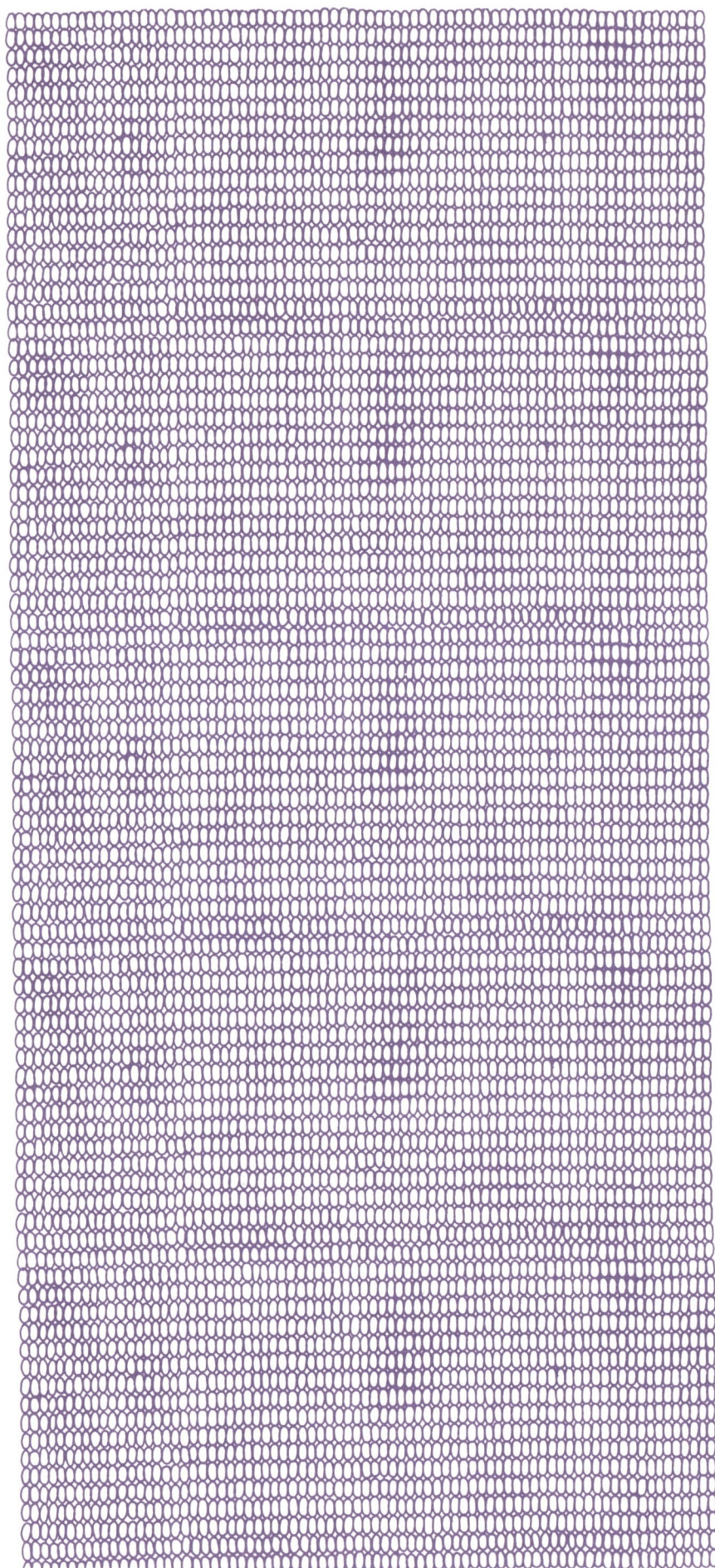

Beadweaving Grids

· Beadweaving Grids ·

· Beadweaving Grids ·

Beadweaving Grids

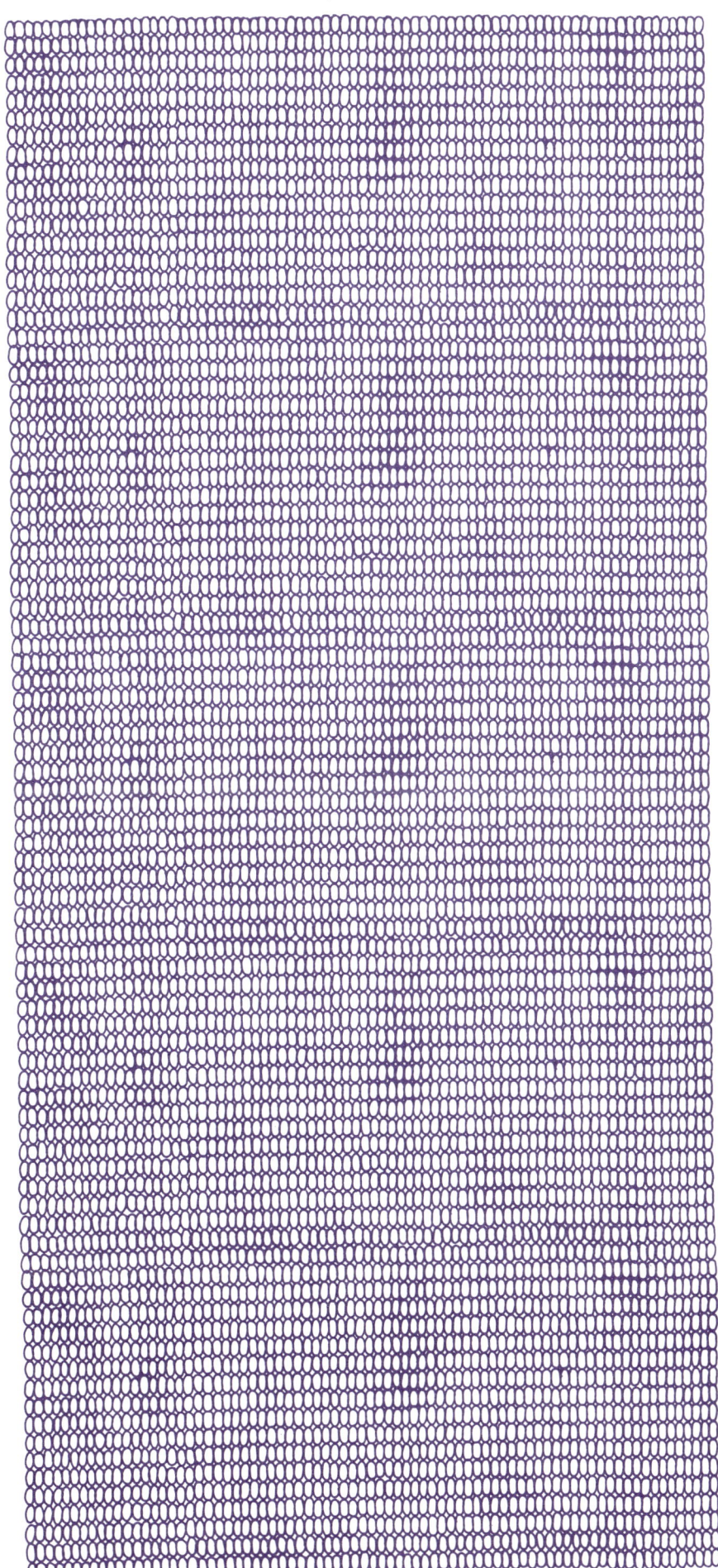

Beadweaving Grids

Beadweaving Grids

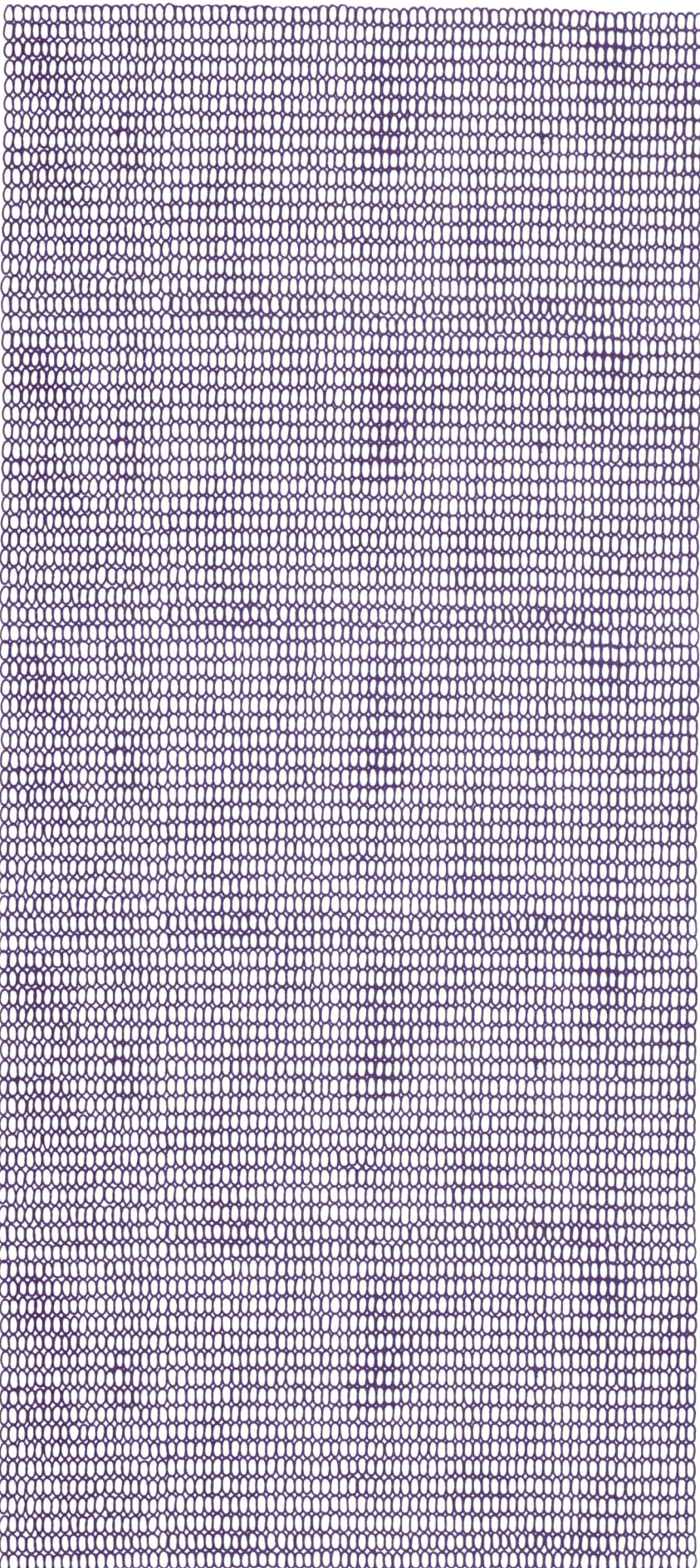

· Beadweaving Grids ·

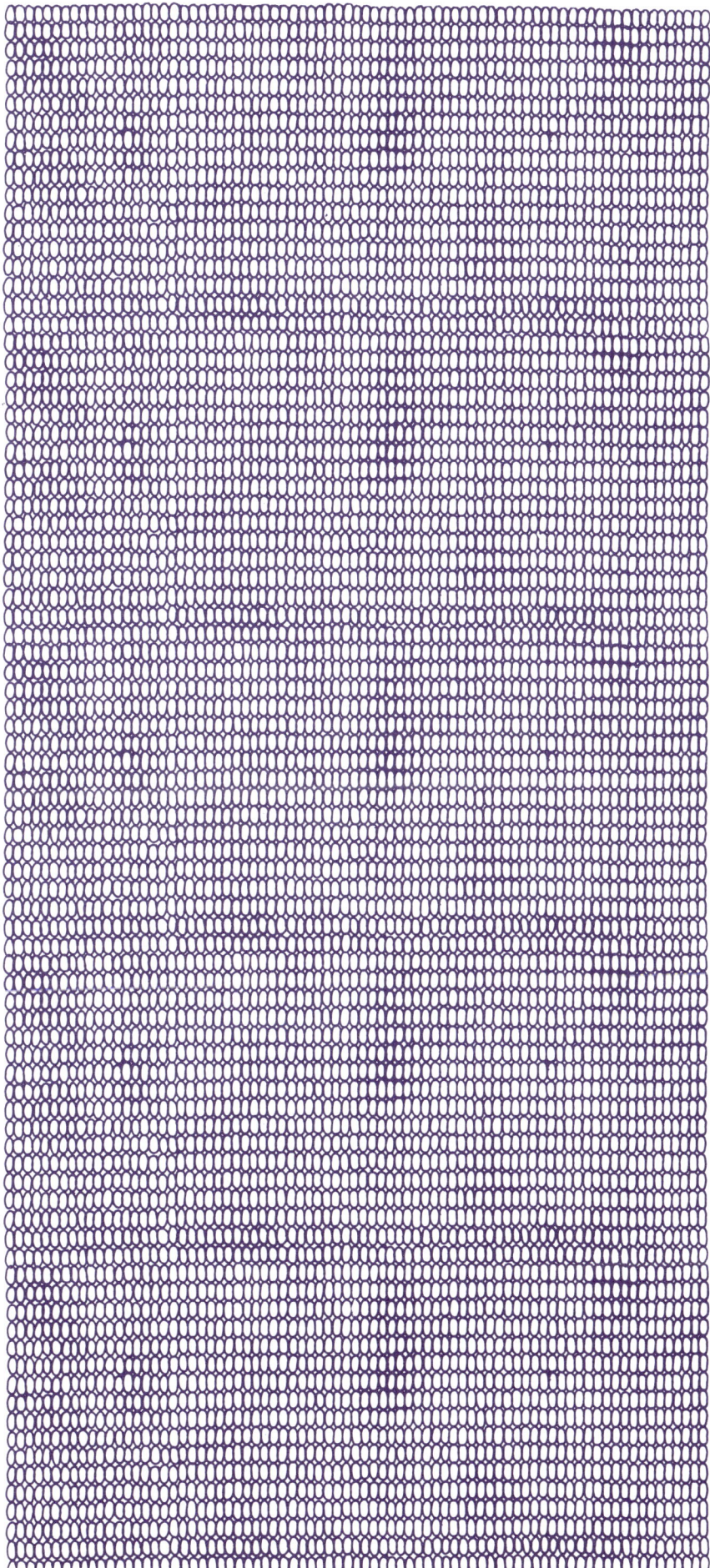

· Beadweaving Grids ·

· Papier Roulé Templates ·

·Papier Roulé Templates·

· Papier Roulé Templates ·